Hamlyn all-colour paperbacks

Howard Linecar

Coins and Medals

illustrated by Bill Stallion
and Harry Perkins

Hamlyn - London
Sun Books - Melbourne

FOREWORD

Having been concerned with numismatics for more than thirty years –
lecturing, writing, publishing, dealing – I know, as every student of
a serious subject soon discovers, that the more one knows the more
there is to be learned. Only if one specializes in some very narrow
field within the whole framework of numismatics, can one hope to
become a leading authority. The general writer can only skim the
surface, hoping that his work may lead others to look more deeply
into the subject.

This book is not offered as a definitive work, but as a general introduction to a vast subject where the work of the true authorities –
Charles Seltman, Harold Mattingly, C. H. V. Sutherland, G. C. Brooke,
H. A. Grueber and hundreds more – provide the landmarks and
guide-lines for those wanting to specialize.

The student of numismatics will almost certainly be a collector of
coins, too. The chapters here on the collecting of coins and the notes
on their care and housing will help the beginner in the shaping of a
collection which should increase in value as it grows in variety and
interest.

H.L.

*The coins illustrated in this book are not all drawn to a common scale.
Where coins are considerably enlarged or reduced, this has been noted
in the captions.*

Published by The Hamlyn Publishing Group Limited
London · New York · Sydney · Toronto
Hamlyn House, Feltham, Middlesex, England
In association with Sun Books Pty Ltd Melbourne

Copyright © The Hamlyn Publishing Group Limited 1971

ISBN 0 600 00122 9
Phototypeset by Filmtype Services Limited, Scarborough
Colour separations by Schwitter Limited, Zurich
Printed in Holland by Smeets, Weert

CONTENTS

The age of barter

Before money as we know it today became the god of mankind, trade was carried on by bartering the commodities necessary to sustain life one against another. With the discovery of gold, sometimes found in an almost unalloyed state, the civilized peoples of the south Mediterranean areas began to hunt for this untarnishable, indestructible metal, to hoard it and to make it into ornaments, vessels and the like. Large hoards of such objects have been found in the tombs of Egyptian kings. Egypt was probably the richest gold-producing area in the ancient world, with two main deposits, in Upper Egypt and in Nubia, both between the Nile and the Red Sea, between about the 26th and 23rd parallels of latitude.

In the Early and Middle Bronze Ages in the Mediterranean area the various peoples surrounding this sea had little contact with one another. The numerous kingdoms and communities were more or less self-supporting. At the beginning of the Late Bronze Age, about 1600 BC, great changes began to take place in the economic conditions of the ancient world. In about 1800 BC various Asiatic tribes had seized Babylonia and overpowered Egypt, which suffered their domination for some 200 years. Then, throwing off the yoke of foreign

domination the Egyptians advanced into Asia in a series of wars of revenge.

Both the Asiatics and the Egyptians had been greatly aided by the use of the horse in their campaigns. With its increasing use, it became possible to guard caravans of goods being transported on the slower camel and donkey by mounting warriors on horseback who could deal swiftly with an attack. Feeling more secure, traders began to venture further afield than before and the peoples of the various states began to meet.

The traders of the Nile and other great river civilizations found that across the sea in Europe and in the highlands and pasturelands of Asia there were many races of people. The wealth of these people lay in their flocks and herds, rather than in the golden metal so much prized among the inhabitants of the south. The northerners almost certainly had a standard of exchange value based on the ox, the cow and the sheep. It is known that the ox was the standard of value among Homer's Achaeans as late as the twelfth century BC.

When the traders of Egypt and Mesopotamia, of the Nile and Babylonia began to come into more frequent contact with those of the Hittites, the Phoenician Semites, with the Cretans and tribesmen from the northern shores of the Aegean Sea it was frequently on islands such as Crete and Cyprus that they met. As on the land, traffic on the sea began to increase. The Egyptians and Semites brought with them manufactured goods: linen and dyed wool in various forms, and rings and other gold objects. The Hittites brought silver and cattle, and the Cypriots, ingots of copper, a metal then as now native to the island.

The babble of many languages at such a market can well be imagined. The difficulties of attempting to barter live cattle, copper ingots, wool and linen goods, gold and silver objects and weapons one against another must have seemed almost beyond solution. While the inanimate objects could sometimes be divided in a convenient way, the live objects could not. Kill the ox or sheep and convert him into beef or mutton and his value at once decreased. There was no method of preserving meat in those ancient times and it soon became useless in a hot climate.

So gradually it came about that the ox, because he could not

Egyptian gold ring
(enlarged)

Cyprus talent,
c. 11th century
(enlarged)

Half talent from Cyprus
(enlarged)

be divided, became a standard of value. He was judged the equal of a recognized amount of gold, silver (less frequently) or copper, or of so many bales of linen or sacks of grain. The first step towards money had been made.

Throughout coinage history weight is important, and never more so than in this period. In the Aegean area the cost of obtaining gold, coupled with availability to traders, led to the evolution of a unit of this metal weighing about 8·5 grammes in modern weight. In form these units took the shape of little gold pellets, bars or rings. In the grave of a Mycenae king, whose dynasty had ruled during the fifteenth and part of the fourteenth centuries BC, were found not only gold rings of the type just mentioned but spirals of gold wire. Some of these appear to have been adjusted to the 8·5 grammes weight of the gold unit or talent, as it was called. Here, then, was another form of exchange unit.

Two points should be noted. First, the word 'talent' frequently used in the Bible: it can now be seen whence the word came and what it represented. Second, the relative absence of silver, partly because it is more easily destructible than gold, which is unaffected by climate, acid or time. The gold objects in the tombs and graves come out as fresh as the day they were buried. Anyone who has brought up silver coins from the ground or from beneath the sea knows that they are usually heavily corroded, often stuck together in lumps. Only with great care can they be separated and frequently many are ruined.

A copper unit also evolved, probably not so much because the metal was more common in some areas, but because it was offered in trade in certain places, particularly Cyprus. Copper being rated in value less lightly than gold, the unit or talent was correspondingly larger. It took the form of a large or cumbersome ingot weighing some $25\frac{1}{2}$ kilogrammes. On the scale of weights then in use in Greece, this was some 3,000 times the weight of the gold talent.

When our unfortunate ox died, or was at last killed for meat, his hide was also of value. The preserving of animal skins, tanning in various forms, goes back to times before civilized man. The usable part of a four-footed animal's skin when carefully removed looks a little like the animal, flattened out. Perhaps it was not coincidence that caused some of the copper talents to take a similar shape. The 5 Mils coin issued in Cyprus in 1955 shows on the reverse an ingot-bearer carrying just such an animal-skin talent.

It would not be correct to assume that the whole of the Mediterranean area had a more or less uniform system of ex-

Copper or bronze talents, such as this bronze one from Mycenae, could weigh more than sixty pounds

change. During the Late Bronze Age the peoples of the northern shores and the islands such as Sardinia, Crete and Cyprus certainly had the ox unit rated at a gold talent of 8·5 grammes. But the ingot of copper, the large and heavy equivalent of both ox and gold, varied in weight since it was so much less easily portable than its gold equivalent.

So far we have only considered 'an ox'. It must have resulted that in dealings of any size, at any rate in the Cyprus 'copper area', the merchant might find himself having to deal with a great weight of copper, not easily shipped or handled. One such talent, now in the British Museum, weighs 37 kilogrammes. In Mycenae, however, copper was scarce and the talents weighed less. Those used by the Achaeans in Greece weighed only about 25½ kilogrammes. The Greeks of a later age used the word talanton, talent, to describe a heavy weight. The whole system was heavy and unwieldy.

On the other side of the Mediterranean the Egyptians formed a second cultural region and Mesopotamia, Syria and Palestine a third. In this third region the people were partly agricultural and partly pastoral. Probably they too had based their dealings on animal units. They had a twofold weight system, with a small and a large unit. The larger unit was the Babylonian gold shekel of about 8·34 grammes and the smaller the biltu, of some 30 kilogrammes of base metal. The Babylonians, good mathematicians, evolved a third weight unit, the manah. This fitted in between the light gold shekel and the heavy base metal biltu on the following system:

1 shekel, weight 8·34 grammes in modern weight
60 shekels = 1 manah, weight 500·40 grammes
60 manah = 1 biltu, weight 30,024·00 grammes.

All these systems and metals and weights and sizes, used at different periods and in different places, had to come together into some sort of recognized system of exchange if the various peoples we have met were, as time passed, to come closer together as traders and merchants. Meantime the wealth accumulated by rulers and merchants had to be kept safely.

Travelling merchants or indeed any traders could not carry about with them large stores of precious gold or great weights of copper talents. Their accumulated wealth began to be stored in strong rooms in palaces or in the temples, whose

Detail from a painting in the tomb of Rekhmire at Thebes, showing gold rings being measured against weights in the form of animal heads. Gold rings, the earliest Egyptian currency in gold, were first produced c. 2720-2270 BC.

sacred function offered protection from thieves. Recorders working with clay tablets kept records by weight of 'payments' and 'withdrawals'. Thus grew up the treasure houses of Egypt and the ancient world and the great wealth of the temples and religious orders. Two more steps had been taken, one towards the evolution of some unit that would be acceptable in general trade anywhere, the other towards banking such a unit when it arrived.

The coin takes shape

Now we see the gold blob of metal, the gold talent, begin to turn itself into a very primitive coin. We have observed how these gold blobs of metal evolved and how they were accepted for international trading purposes in the Ancient Mediterranean world. So far had this international trade developed that a need arose for some unit of exchange which would be accepted as of incontrovertible value. Someone had to say, in affect, 'This piece of gold is of the same value as your ox. Among friendly traders this we know. Trade is growing. We need a piece of gold marked in such a way that it will be accepted not only by our friends but by other traders. Whoever offers this piece of gold will then know it again and accept it when it is returned to him, though it may have passed through many hands.' How then to mark the piece of gold?

There is no documentary proof but long consideration of the matter, coupled with finds of such pieces, has brought forth the conclusion that the gold talent was marked with rough indentations. This marking is thought to have been done in a very simple way. A bronze nail was part cut through. It was then broken in half. One half, probably the upper part, was used as a punch. A sharp blow with a hammer impressed the nail-mark on the gold talent.

Two Asiatic electrum 'dumps' (enlarged) dating from the 7th century BC. Their markings were almost certainly made with a broken nail.

Broken iron nails hammered on to pieces of metal, or 'dumps', produced the first crude, but individually marked coins

The idea, whoever thought of it, was quite clever. It was not very likely that any two nails part cut and then broken through would produce the same profile and thus make exactly the same mark on the metal. The nail-mark theory is accepted by many numismatists, but it still poses a number of questions. First, how old is the nail? Second, where did bronze come from?

In considering such questions we must appreciate the knowledge and intelligence of these people of the remote past. It is all too easy from the modern standpoint of our own achievements to look upon them as primitives, grubbing about in the dust. This they were not. The legacy which they have left us of their achievements in the form of fine buildings, now in ruins, is but one instance that proves the contrary in a form which any traveller to the Ancient World can see.

The distinction between the great civilizations of the past

and those of the present is partly that those of the past achieved what they achieved by direct manpower, often slave labour, which was cheap 3,000 years ago. Brain power and man power between them built the Ancient World, whereas brain power and increasing mechanical power built the Modern. This is not to say that the builders of the Ancient World had no mechanical aids at all. They had the pulley-block, the primitive crane and they made use of the gradient.

They had also an increasing knowledge of the relatively small number of metals at their command. In Egypt there was plenty of gold, though often too soft for the uses to which it was put. They learned to alloy it with stronger metals. In Cyprus, there was plenty of copper, again too soft for use on its own, in construction, so it was alloyed to produce bronze. So long as two pieces of wood had to be joined together for construction a pin was needed, the nail. Bronze nails were known in the Ancient World. So we have our cut nail as a primitive die, marking the trader's gold talent which he offered in trade and would be prepared to recognize if and when it was returned to him.

This is the theory. In practice it would not be so simple. The roughly marked gold talent would not be instantly recognizable as soon as several people began to make use of the idea. Many would resemble each other sufficiently to cause muddle and delay in transacting business. The first step towards making a coin had been taken, but the problem was still not solved.

It is said that this marking system probably had its origins in Ionia. At this period there were fairly close trading relationships between Ionia and Lydia; both employed the same monetary systems when they first started to make use of coins.

At this period, and we are coming now to circa 1,000-700 BC, it was the custom for an oriental potentate to sign a written document with the application of a seal bearing his private device. From there it was only a matter of time before someone hit upon the idea of placing his private seal-mark on his talents of gold, though we shall probably never know who first did so.

Then came the next two steps. Seeing the seal-mark on certain gold talents, why not cut some device on the broken nail? Further, since the piece of metal had to be placed on a solid surface while it was being stamped with the mark, why not mark that surface also with some device cut into it which would produce the said device in relief on the metal? Finally, to make the whole operation easier, why not soften the metal by heating it?

The moment when the first of these two and probably the third operation came together was the moment of the birth of the coin. The blobs of metal began to take on a more carefully calculated weight and, being privately marked and so at once recognized, need not be checked for weight again. As they passed in trade among merchants and tradesmen their mark was their guarantee.

This is all very simplified, but it was probably along these lines that, somewhere about 700 BC, coins came into being. Their development and progress we shall see in the following chapters.

Designs on Ionian electrum coins were varied (*From the top*): stag, horse's head, lion scalps, winged bull. (The coins are all illustrated enlarged.)

Greek silver coins. (*Left*) Aegina two-drachm coin, 7th century BC; the obverse design is a turtle. (*Centre*) Corinthian stater, *c.* 600 BC, with Pegasus on the obverse. (*Right*) 7th century BC Corinthian stater. (These coins are illustrated enlarged.)

Art steps in

We now have coins, though they are primitive in many ways. They are still very limited in their use in what, to us, is a small world of commerce, the lands around the Mediterranean Sea. Now the artist begins to step in and to make something of the coin as an art form. To see how this happened we must look at the civilizations of Ancient Greece.

Before we do so it must be made absolutely clear that, while we are making some attempt to show how coins developed, we are not following the matter through in a numismatically logical and chronological manner. The last dates given were 1,000-700 BC. They were mentioned in order to give some idea of how long ago actual coins evolved. Now, by starting to consider the coins of Ancient Greece, we are hedge-hopping time.

In recent years a number of countries such as Australia have determined the course of history by saying, 'This is the last day on which we use pounds, shillings and pence. Tomorrow we change to dollars and cents.' There was no point in time in which the Ancient World said, 'This is the last day on which we use coins marked by the nail and the seal, tomorrow we change over to fine artistic designs.' Such designs evolved very gradually.

Ancient Greece, more properly called the Hellenic world, evolved itself into a number of city-states. Imagine your country as a series of self-contained regions having no overall government or central authority, and some idea of the Greek city-state can be discerned.

It should be pointed out that the Greek city-states were not confined to the mainland of Greece. Though situated mainly on the coast, they were founded as far away as the western end of Sicily, as far as Massalia on what is now the south coast of France, on the shores of the Black Sea and in Asia Minor.

The Greek city-states came into being following a series of migrations of Hellenic people who populated the peninsula of Greece. The greatest of these migrations, the Dorian invasion, took the Greek invaders not only well into the south of Greece but overseas as well. Out of these migrations and invasions there gradually grew the city-states, some of whose names are familiar to most of us. Athens, probably the best known, became the centre of government for Attica. Sparta, too, we know, and such names as Corinth, Megara and Thebes. On the Aegean islands states were also developing, and away in Asia Minor the great commercial city-states were founded. As well as Sicily, southern Italy had many city-states and there were trading posts on the north African coast. Here the Phoenicians held on to Carthage and remained a thorn in the Greek side and a constant challenge. There were also many other city-states whose names are more familiar to historians, and trading posts over the whole area.

Nearly all of these city-states and communities were completely independent, making their own policies, fighting each other at times and in general going their own way. Some of them might combine at a time of common danger, only to break up again and perhaps war with each other once the danger was passed.

Several centuries passed in this way. Because the city-states never combined permanently their world began to fall to pieces. In Sicily the Greeks were never in full control, being menaced by the native Sicels and Sicians from the interior of the island and by the hostile Carthaginians from without and from their foothold on the western tip of the island. In 490 BC the Persians crossed the Aegean Sea, landed at Marathon and invaded Attica. The Spartans sent help, which arrived too late. The victory of Marathon was almost entirely Athenian.

A second great invasion by the Persians under Xerxes took place in 480 BC. This time the army sent by the Spartans to help was wiped out at Thermopylae and Athens was evacuated and occupied by the enemy. Then the sea victory of Salamis again reversed the situation. In 431 BC the Peloponnesian War broke out. This lasted twenty-seven years and so weakened both sides that the military adventurer, King Philip of Macedon, a Greek with a completely un-Hellenic outlook, and his son, Alexander, between them destroyed for ever the civilization of the city states.

Yet, strange as it may seem, it was during the long period

(*Left*) Athens silver ten-drachm piece, *c.* 485 BC, has Athena on the obverse and an owl on the reverse. (*Right*) silver ten-drachm coin from Syracuse, *c.* 479 BC, with a chariot design on the obverse and a head on the reverse.

when the city-states plotted, murdered and bribed each other that all the best of what was Greece was achieved. Scientific medicine, mathematics, astronomy, biology, painting, music, sculpture, architecture: all this and much more reached great heights of development.

While Greek fought Greek, while the Persians intrigued and invaded, while the Carthaginians attacked in the west and the Greek civilization seemed to be crumbling, fine coins were developing and being minted.

Failing to unite as a whole, almost endless combinations of city-states were formed to fight other such combinations as well as invaders. Finally, when Philip of Macedon came to the throne in 359 BC and began his activities aimed at the domination of the Hellenic world a great deal of his work had been done for him.

The shadows now begin to lengthen. Sixteen terrible years saw Athens crushed at last in 338 BC. In 336 BC Philip died. Hope rose for a time, only to be dashed by the campaigns of Alexander. The city-states were now too weak even to delay the main object of the campaigns, the subjugation of the east. With the death of Alexander in 322 BC and the flight and suicide of Demosthenes, Athenian opponent of both Philip and his son, the political life of the Greek city-states fell apart for ever. In the twilight of an uneasy period of history when Macedonian generals ruled in Asia Minor and Egypt, the Hellenic world waited, at first unconsciously, its absorption into the Roman world.

Coins had developed considerably during this period. The artist, the designer and the die cutter had long begun to make their influence felt. In Terentum and Sicily, to name but two places, artists had begun to put their signatures on their coin designs by 400 BC. The final appearance of a coin, within broad limits, was left to the artist. Being told that a coin should have on one side the emblem of some Greek city-state and that on the reverse it should have a triumphal chariot, the artist was left to translate this into fact.

We now see how this worked out. In the midst of this ever-uneasy Hellenic world the finest coins ever seen were designed and struck. 'War', said the Greek philosopher Heracleitus, 'is the father of all and the king of all.'

The obverse of a
Roman bronze coin,
struck *c.* 235 BC.
(enlarged)

The further spread of coinage

Now that coins are established, how did their use continue to
spread? To the west had begun the rise of the Roman world.
Their government was to dominate the known world and to
give the basis of many of the laws under which we still live.

While the Hellenic world broke up because it failed to
unite, it can, perhaps, be said that the Roman world survived
so long and had such power as it attained because it was a unit.
In the days of its greatest power everything centred on Rome,
the hub of the wheel. So far as coinage is concerned its spread
into the then known world was similar to the rings produced
when a stone is cast into a pool of water. As the Roman world
expanded, taking in such territories as Greece, North Africa,
Palestine, Spain, France (Gaul) and ultimately Britain, so the
use of its coins spread.

This development occurred in an uneven way. The colonies

Three Roman coins. (*From left*) sextans, *c.* 235 BC; gold
six-scruples piece, 217 BC; dodrans, *c.* 121 BC.

of Greece, some of them in Italy, already had a coinage of the fine types which we have seen. To the north of Rome Etruria also began to make use of coinage about 500 BC, although if there was any coinage in the less developed parts of Italy it took the form of large, chunky pieces known as Aes Rude, having no mark of value. They were followed by cast bronze bars, first of irregular weight but later trimmed to weigh about five pounds. Known as Aes Signatum they had something of a design on either side and were used probably about 289 BC, when a form of 'currency board' was set up in Rome.

Next came another heavy cast bronze piece, the Aes Grave, circular and with a design on both sides. These pieces carried a mark of value and were based on the As. The following scale of relationships was then established:

As = 1 pound, mark of value l
Semis = $\frac{1}{2}$ pound, mark of value S
Quincunx = 5 ounces, mark of value . . . . .
Tremis = 4 ounces, mark of value . . . .
Quadrans = 3 ounces, mark of value . . .
Sextans = 2 ounces, mark of value . .
Uncia (ounce) = 1 ounce, mark of value .

The pound was divided into twelve ounces: thus three Tremis equalled one As. It will be noted that, as before, the coins were directly allied to weight standards. This system remained sufficient to meet the internal requirements of Rome so long as she remained only a central Italian state. Once she began to conquer her neighbours the clumsy Aes Grave were no longer suitable as coinage.

A silver coinage was devised which was acceptable in the

Gold aureaus with Nero on the obverse, c. AD 66 (enlarged)

states of central Italy and in the Greek cities of Italy with which expanding Rome came into contact. Over several decades a series of silver coins of varying types appeared, with the reverse inscription ROMA or ROMANO: i.e. Romanorum, of the Romans.

As the power of Rome grew a great change became possible. Strong enough now to assert her authority in such matters she no longer had to accommodate her coinage to suit that of her neighbours. She was ready to inaugurate, in about 211 BC, an entirely new monetary system which Italy was bound to accept.

The new system comprised three denominations of silver, the denarius, the quinarius (= half-denarius) and the sestertius (= quarter-denarius). Seven denominations of struck bronze coins (as opposed to the cast pieces seen so far) followed the silver pieces. The names were the same as those in the table of the cast pieces given above, but a semuncia or half-ounce was added. This represents the basic monetary system of

Roman coins. (*Top*) antoninianus with head of Caracalla on obverse; (*centre*) eight-denarius piece; (*bottom*) double solidus c. AD 393, gold.

Four coins used by the Ancient Britons. The large stater (*left*) dates from the Gallo-Belgic invasion of *c.* 125 BC.

the Roman Republic down to about the last thirty to fifty years of its existence. There are small numbers of rare gold coins, mainly struck from metal acquired through war or received as tribute. The established 'currency board', the *Tresviri* or 'three men' concerned with the casting and striking of gold, silver and bronze, continued to provide the coins.

Another great change was to be made in the Roman monetary system when the Roman Empire developed. In the last years of the Republic, in the period of the civil wars and the bitter struggle for control of the city of Rome, the various contestants began to place their portraits on the coins which they themselves caused to be struck for their respective armies. Caesar, Brutus, Pompey, Mark Antony and Octavian all appeared on coins. The latter eventually took the name of Augustus and became the first Roman Emperor.

A few years before the beginning of the Christian era Augustus completely reformed the monetary system. Gold coins, known as aurei ('gold coins') began to appear regularly. The denominations were as follows:

    1 aureus = 25 denarii

1 quinarius aureus (or $\frac{1}{2}$ aureus) = $12\frac{1}{2}$ denarii

1 denarius = 4 brass sestertii

1 quinarius (silver) = 2 brass sestertii

1 sestertius = 4 copper asses = 2 brass dupondii

1 dupondius = 2 copper asses

1 as = 4 copper quadrantes (or $\frac{1}{4}$ asses).

This system lasted with minor changes for some two centuries until the time of the Emperor Caracalla, AD 211-217, when a new denomination appeared, the antoninianus, named after him.

Before Rome achieved her ascendancy, previous coinages also reached far and wide. When Julius Caesar reached Britain, 55-54 BC, he found in use what might broadly be called a series of 'run down' coins. Some of them were based on the Stater of Philip of Macedon. This series of coins as a whole is broadly referred to as the 'Ancient British', and was used by various tribes.

Very broadly, the various coins in use from the time of Ancient Greece until the fourteenth century AD were produced by two methods, casting and striking by hand. In Ancient Britain there was a small series of cast pieces, some of which were found in Kent. Striking coins by hand was found for various reasons to be much the more practical. We saw how this started in Ancient Greece with the anvil and the nail, engraved to make dies. In Anglo-Saxon, Norman and later England, where many mints were in operation, the process was brought to its final development before machines began to take over coin production.

The more important towns and burghs, each largely self-sufficient and rather isolated, minted their own coins. As the country developed the number of mints declined and government became more centralized. The final centralization of the Royal Mint in London, at that time in the Tower, came with the reign of Charles II, 1660-85, though branch mints have been used since on various occasions for special purposes. This reign also saw machine-made coins put into general circulation in Britain for the first time.

Tin coins being cast in Ancient Britain. A notable hoard of such coins was found in Kent in southern England.

British coins – the first mechanical revolution

After some 2,200 years of striking coins by hand the age of the mechanically produced coin began to dawn. Primitive machines were put to work and what is known as the milled series of coins began to appear. Coins made with the help of machines reached England, later Britain, from the Continent. A few coins produced by the 'mill and screw press' were struck in the reign of Elizabeth I (1558-1603). At this time the mechanical method of coin production was uneconomic, for various reasons into which we need not delve, and the idea of coins produced with the aid of primitive machines lapsed. In the reign of Charles I (1625-49), two small issues of milled or machine-made coins were struck. These coins were fine pieces and gave some idea of what could be produced with the help of primitive machines. But for the Civil War, further issues might well have appeared.

During the Commonwealth period (1649-60), hammered coins continued to be struck. When Cromwell was styled Lord Protector a series of milled coins was prepared. Those which were struck are

Horses were used to drive the two rolling mills in the Tower of London mint. Each mill had two horizontal iron cylinders like a domestic mangle, which were driven via wooden gears by the horses tramping round a capstan below. The rollers were surprisingly small – only 4 inches in diameter.

now usually considered as pattern pieces since it is doubtful
if they were ever circulated.

From 1660-62 (Charles II), hammered coins were still struck
while various experiments prepared the way for the introduction of the new milled money. Artists and engravers produced pattern and trial pieces. Mr Pepys makes mention of
them in his Diary.

The whole question of machinery in any form revolves on
a source of power. In the reign of Charles II there was only
water, wind and horse power. Though windmills crowned
many hills, as a source of power they made no great contribution to coin production. Water was, for a short time,

(*Top*) Henry VII gold ryal.
(*Bottom*) silver groat of Henry V.
The obverse portrait is not the
king's; variations of it were on
coins from Edward I to
Richard III.

harnessed to drive machines,
but again contributed little to
the advance of minting machinery. Very broadly, from
1662 till the closing years of
the eighteenth century, it was
the horse who provided coin-
making power.

His contribution consisted
in driving mills, like large
mangles, through whose rollers the metal passed to reduce
it to an even thickness. He
was harnessed to what was in
affect a large capstan and, by
walking in a circular track,
in a basement below the
Tower Mint, drove a large
crown-wheel. Squirrel-cage
pinions, mounted on axles at
right angles to the crown-
wheel, transmitted the horse
power through further axles
to the rollers. The strips of
metal then produced had circular blanks cut out of them
in much the same way as one
cuts dough to make a jam tart.
The thickness of the blanks
was greater than those previously used for hammered
coins, so that the size of the
coins was in many cases reduced in diameter to compensate for the extra thickness.

The blanks were then
passed to a man who operated
a machine which marked the
edges with lettering or graining. This consisted of two

bars, one fixed to a bench and one which moved parallel to the fixed bar when the operator turned a handle. Lettering was cut incuse on one of the bars. When the circular blank was placed between them and the handle was turned, the blank revolved between the bars and emerged with raised lettering or graining on its edge.

The lettered or grained blank then went to a screw press. In the bedplate was the die for the obverse of the coin, complete with portrait and lettering. Fixed to the axle of the screw press above, was the reverse die, complete with design and lettering. Operators then hauled on ropes connected to the weighted arms of the press, the axle descended on a screw and the upper die struck the flan, or blank, placed in position on the lower die. The metal 'flowed' into the incuse channels of the designs of both upper and lower dies, marked the blank and produced the finished coin. Later a collar was devised with lettering or graining on it.

(*Above*) gold milled half-pound of Elizabeth I. (*Below*) Oliver Cromwell appears on the obverse of this 1658 silver crown.

27

This confined the coin at the moment of striking and produced the edge marking at the same time as the main device was produced on the obverse and reverse of the blank.

Improvements went on all the time. At first the edge-marking machine had only one bar lettered, so that the blank had to complete a revolution between the two bars to receive the whole of the marking. Later, half the legend was placed on each of the two bars. The blank then had to make only half a revolution. Then came the collar mentioned above.

While two men could work the press for small coins, as many as twelve might be needed to produce the larger pieces. In general four men was an adequate number. A further operator sat in a shallow pit in the floor. His work was to knock out the coin from the press when it had been struck and insert another previously edged blank, passed to him from the

Man-power, instead of horse-power, operated this Swedish hammer-press marking plate money

Despite its size, this coining press could strike one coin every two seconds

edge lettering press. This method of producing coins, always under review, frequently subjected to improvement and development, produced the coins in use in England from the reign of Charles II till the latter years of the reign of George III (1760-1820).

Coins – money – now passed more frequently into the hands of the general public. The 'man in the field' was becoming the 'man in the street'. The range of Charles II coins consisted of gold five, two, one and half-guinea pieces. In silver were the crown, halfcrown, shilling, sixpence, fourpence, threepence, twopence and penny. Copper halfpence were added.

Experiments with copper pieces of small denomination had been carried on from the time of Elizabeth I. The origins of the bronze (once copper) coins of today had their roots in a second mechanical revolution which is the next part of our story.

Further improvements in minting

Coins continued to be produced by the methods we have been looking at from 1662 to 1816. It has already been said that the Royal Mint had been in the Tower of London from about the time it was built in roughly its present form. English, later British, money was struck there till the Mint keys were formally handed to the Constable of the Tower of London in August 1812.

Towards the end of the eighteenth century various circumstances which finally resulted in the removal of the Mint began to come together. For economic reasons the coinage of Britain had fallen into a bad state. At the same time methods of coin production had become outdated and the whole matter came under the review of the Committee on Coin.

As the Committee was moving towards coinage reform, a new force was about to arrive in the coinage world – Matthew Boulton. In 1745, when he was seventeen, Matthew had entered the family business in Birmingham. A man of a most inventive turn of mind, he gradually improved the products them-

Machinery from Matthew Boulton's Soho mint was bought by the Birmingham firm of Ralph Heaton and Sons and used by them until the late 19th century. This picture shows some of Boulton's steam coining presses in use at Ralph Heaton's in 1862. Boulton's earliest steam presses were constructed in 1786. Russia bought a set of his machines in 1799 and thus became the first state to own steam coining plant.

selves as well as the methods of their manufacture.

In 1759 at the age of thirty-one Matthew Boulton took over his father's business, and in 1762 he built the Soho Manufactory in the district of that name in the township of Handsworth, then on the outskirts of Birmingham. In 1767, now under the royal patronage of George III, he extended the Manufactory and in the next year met James Watt for the first time. In 1774 he acquired an interest in Watt's steam engine patent, persuaded Watt to come to Birmingham and the next year went into partnership with him for a term of twenty-five years, Watt's patent being extended for a similar term.

In the midst of many other interests Boulton took up coinage. In part this was because the copper coins, what there were of them, consisted of an inadequate number of halfpence and farthings; the need for a minor coinage in base metal was great, and private traders were issuing tokens. Coin forgeries were

British copper coinage of George III's reign. (*Top*) twopence and halfpenny. (*Bottom*) farthing and penny.

also common, partly because of their irregular shape. While stressing to the government of the day the need for a coinage which was better produced, and the need for a proper base-metal issue, Boulton set about improving minting machinery. He applied steam power to coining in 1786, appeared before the Privy Council, then concerning itself with coinage matters, in 1788, took out a patent for a coining press in 1790 and in 1797, at the age of sixty-nine, received a contract for a British copper coinage, the ancestor of the bronze pieces which the United Kingdom uses today.

The Committee on Coin inspected the Royal Mint in 1798. For advice they called in John Rennie, FRS, who had worked for Boulton and Watt. Rennie's report on the state of affairs at the Mint was delivered in trenchant terms in July 1798. Briefly, little or nothing was right: methods, machines and equipment were out of date. Rennie came down on the side of steam power and more steam power to drive modern machinery. By this time both he and the rest of the country knew what this new steam coining machinery could do. They had Boulton's regal copper coinage in their hands.

Modern minting machinery, though complex, does not require the same man-power as did the mills and presses of earlier centuries

By 1804 the Committee on Coin had been converted to steam power. It was agreed that the Royal Mint should move and in 1812 it went to the fine buildings, later extended many times, on Little Tower Hill, where it stayed until its removal to Wales in 1969. Boulton and Watt supplied the machinery. During the period of transition (1807-12) operators were sent to Birmingham to learn how to use it. The equipment exactly duplicated that of Boulton's private Birmingham mint, save that in the Royal Mint there were twelve blank-cutting presses instead of the eight in Boulton's.

Power was provided by four rotative steam engines which drew their water from the Tower moat, then still full. One engine of thirty horse-power drove three rolling mills. The first mill broke down the metal ingots, the second flattened the strips so produced still further, and the third completed their reduction, providing what are known as fillets from which the blanks are cut.

Next came a sixteen horse-power engine which drove twelve blank-cutting presses. The third steam engine, this time of ten horse-power, drove eight coining presses. Each

Molten coinage alloy is poured into moulds to form the bars from which the coins will eventually be cut

press had two airtight cylinders and the revolving of an over-head horizontal wheel drew the pistons upwards. The vacuum force so created caused the pistons sharply to descend. This recoil action drove pivots which turned a heavily loaded bar. This in turn drove a spiralled column with the reverse die on the end, causing the die to strike the blank placed below. Each press struck sixty coins a minute. Finally, a six horse-power engine drove a variety of die-turning lathes and milling, shaking and pulverizing machinery.

With all this new equipment came a further reform in the coinage. Coins were now absolutely circular in shape and accurate in weight. In the gold range sovereigns and half-sovereigns replaced the guineas and their halves. The silver range was the same, crown to Maundy penny. With the exception of the four Maundy pieces, which still carried on their reverses the crowned figures, 4, 3, 2, 1 respectively, new designs were used. William Wellesley-Pole, later Lord Mornington (elder brother of the famous Duke of Wellington) as Master of the new Mint was so enamoured of a design of St

The cast bars go through several 'rolling down' stages to bring them to coin thickness

George and the dragon, by an Italian, Benedetto Pistrucci, that he invited the artist to design the new coinage and adopted the St George as the reverse design for the sovereign and the crown. This design has come and gone over the last century and a half and is with us still on the sovereigns of Elizabeth II.

The new machinery and production methods continued in use in much their original form till the 1870s, by which time they were both outdated and worn out.

The Boulton process of coin striking relied on a great hammer-blow by the coining press to produce the finished coin. In 1839 a German, Uhlhorn, had invented a coining press which, improved by the Frenchman, Thonnelier, produced coins by a squeezing action, by the use of energy stored in a heavy flywheel. Such presses had been installed in branches of the Royal Mint in Sydney and Melbourne when these mints were created in 1853 and 1869 respectively.

It was soon found that the new presses struck one hundred coins a minute, that the dies, always expensive to produce, lasted longer and that the machines made less noise. Between

1872-8 four Uhlhorn presses on hire to the Royal Mint were purchased outright. No further heavy expenditure was allowed. The matter of moving the Mint was once more under discussion.

This idea was at last quashed in 1881 and once more the Mint set about a reorganization. Half a million in silver coin was struck for stock, gold coinage was temporarily at a standstill, the striking of bronze coinage was sub-contracted as was colonial coinage and, on 1 February 1882, the Mint stopped work for ten months.

Extensive and drastic rebuilding and refitting took place. This was in some wise repeated in 1904, 1909-1912 and 1924, the final version lasting until the Royal Mint's removal to Wales.

We have spent a considerable time tracing how coins were made by various mechanical means. We should now look a little more closely at some of the later coins. To do so we will retrace our steps to 1662, the year of the first mechanical revolution in British coinage.

The simplified series of denominations then produced were: Gold: five guineas, two guineas, guinea, half guinea.

(*Left*) among the machinery at the new Royal Australian Mint in Canberra, built at a cost of $A9,000,000, is this press which stamps out coin blanks

Silver: crown, halfcrown, shilling, sixpence, fourpence, threepence, twopence, penny.

Copper (sometimes tin): halfpenny, farthing.

The five guineas were large, satisfying pieces of gold. It is doubtful if they were extensively used in general circulation. Some of the gold was supplied by the Africa Company, and some of the pieces struck from such metal had a small elephant, or an elephant and castle, under the bust. The reverse design consisted of four crowned shields of arms, of England, Scotland, France and Ireland, the third referring to former French possessions, the last of which was lost in 1558. Between the shields were four sceptres in saltire, that is set X-wise, while four interlinked C's formed the centre.

Very similar pieces of the same denomination were struck in the next reign, that of James II (1685-8) but with no C's in the centre. In the next reign, that of William and Mary (1688-94), for the first time since Philip and Mary (1554-8) there were two heads on the obverse depicting the joint monarchs. The reverse had a large complicated shield of arms, crowned and including the shield of Nassau, William's arms, in the centre. When Mary died and William reigned alone (1694-1702), only

The edge of the coin blank is raised in this marking machine

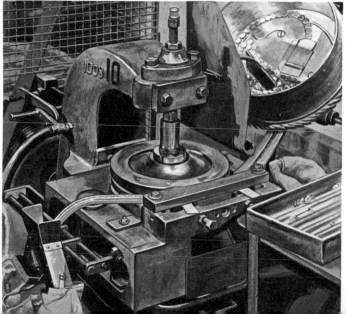

his head appeared on the obverse. The reverse was four shields and sceptres, the shield of Nassau forming the centre.

This type of reverse continued into the reign of Anne (1702-14), a rose forming the centre. The arms had to be varied to include the Scottish shield after the Act uniting the kingdoms of England and Scotland in 1706. This was halved with the English arms on the first and third shields. The arms of France might well have been dropped in favour of those of Scotland. The Star of the Most Noble Order of the Garter then formed the centre. A very rare five guineas of 1703, of which only about fifteen pieces are known, has the word VIGO under the bust. Its presence signifies that these pieces were struck from bullion captured by the combined English and Dutch fleets from the French and Spanish at the Battle of Vigo Bay in 1702.

When George I (1714-27) succeeded to the throne, the four shields of arms again had to be altered. They were now England and Scotland, France (still clung to), Ireland and the Electorate. The king's resounding titles were so lengthy that in the legends they had in some words to be abbreviated to one letter. They were, of course, in Latin and translated in full read GEORGE I BY THE GRACE OF GOD OF GREAT BRITAIN FRANCE AND IRELAND KING DEFENDER OF THE FAITH DUKE OF BRUNSWICK AND LUNEBURG ARCHTREASURER OF THE HOLY ROMAN EMPIRE AND ELECTOR.

The four shields of arms gave place to a large crowned shield on the five guineas of George II (1727-60). It should be pointed out that in many reigns, such as those of Charles II, James II, Anne and George II, more than one type of bust appears. Variations to the bust are usually made in a long reign as the monarch gets older. In the case of George II there were two busts. In 1729 the letters EIC appeared under the king's bust on some pieces, showing that the metal was provided by the East India Company. On the five guineas of 1746 and on certain of the silver coins of 1745 and 1746 the word LIMA appears below the bust. This has a connection with Admiral Anson and his round-the-world voyage of 1740-4, but the significance of the word is doubtful since, under his instructions to disrupt Spanish shipping in the Pacific, he did not attack Lima. In fact the bullion Anson brought back came from a Spanish plate ship on its annual trip from Acapulco to

(*Left*) after being cleaned and washed, coin blanks are dried by hot air in rotating barrels. (*Below*) this machine, striking two coins at a time, can produce 400 coins a minute.

British coins. (*From the top*)
George III 'bull head' halfcrown;
George IV shilling; obverse of the
'godless' Victoria florin, 1849;
Victoria sixpence, 1838.

Manila. It seems probable that this bullion was mixed with other metal captured by free-booters from Spanish plate ships in the Atlantic.

There were no five guinea pieces in the range of the coinage of George III (1760-1820) and this denomination was not struck again.

Over this period of some 140 years the two guineas, guineas and half guineas followed in the main the design of the five guinea pieces. The name guinea, incidentally, originated with the fact that much of the gold from which British coinage at this period was struck came from Guinea in Africa, now Ghana, and from the Gold Coast in general. It was originally supplied by the Africa Company and the East India Company.

A word should be said about the guineas of George III, since they are those with which the collector is most likely to come into contact. They are now quite rare, but not so rare as the gold denominations of earlier reigns. They appeared with six different busts during the long reign and with four different reverse types. Of them all the so-called Spade guinea was by far the most common. It took its name from the plain crowned shield on the reverse which is in the shape of a trenching spade. It first appeared in 1787.

We can next take a look at the silver coinage of the same period. Here collecting interest centres mainly round the crown. The crowns of Charles II looked much like the five guineas, but two C's interlinked take the place of the sceptres. Again there are different busts in this and many other reigns. The crowns of James II were much the same as those of his brother, Charles II, but without the C's. William and Mary still had the four crowned shields of arms on the reverse with the monogram WM in the angles, but complicated matters by having the figures of the date also in the angles. In 1692 this odd way of showing the date caused the die engraver some trouble. As a result pieces exist with the 2 in the date recut over a 2 which is upside down.

In the reign of William III the date on the coinage returned to its traditional place.

(From the top) gold £5, 1839; William IV half sovereign, 1831; George VI half sovereign; George V £2, 1911; Victoria half sovereign, 1838

It was during this reign that the last of the hammered coinage, now very worn and defaced, was called in. To compensate for this more milled coins had to be produced. Branch mints were opened at Bristol, Chester, Exeter, Norwich and York. The initial letters of these mints appear on the coins which were struck, placed below the bust of the king. The crown had no such marks and was not struck in the branch mints.

The crowns struck in the reign of Anne had the same alteration to the shields of arms after the Act of Union as did all the other coins. Now the three-feather symbol and a rose began to appear in the spaces between the shields. The feathers, known as plumes, first appeared in the milled coinage range on the later halfcrowns of William III, and they, with the rose, signified that the silver they were made of came from mines in Wales and England.

The silver coins of George I, except for the Maundy coins, continued the four shields of arms, amended to take in the Electorate. Roses and plumes continued to appear in the angles

Obverse of the Charles II five-guinea gold piece (enlarged). The elephant symbol indicates gold imported from the Africa Company.

but in 1723 they were replaced by the letters SSC. This meant that the metal was supplied by the South Sea Company. Some of the shillings had WCC under the bust and/or CC on the reverse alternating with plumes, meaning that the silver was supplied by the Welsh Copper Company.

The crowns and other silver pieces of George II, again excepting the Maundy coins, continued with the four-shields reverse, with roses and plumes, or roses only, in the angles in various years. There were two bust types. No crowns were struck for George III till after the removal of the Royal Mint from the Tower. Only shillings and sixpences still had the four shields reverse. The reform of the milled coinage under George III produced the following denominations:

Gold: five pounds (probably never circulated); two pounds (probably never circulated); sovereign (£1); and half sovereign (10s.)

(*From the top*) reverse of the Charles II five guineas; William and Mary halfcrown; reverse of a William III halfcrown, the plumes indicating that the silver came from Wales

Queen Anne five-guinea pieces:
reverse. 1793, before Union with
Scotland; obverse, 1705; reverse
1706, after Union

Silver: crown, halfcrown, florin (1849 and after), shilling, sixpence, fourpence, threepence, twopence, penny

Copper (later bronze): penny, halfpenny, farthing.

The five and two pound pieces which probably never circulated were the logical descendants of the five and two guinea pieces. However, only patterns, proofs or very small numbers of these coins have appeared to date. Even when these were struck apparently for circulation they were probably never so used.

Until the coinage reform mentioned above the guinea was the unit gold piece in daily use, its value after several fluctuations being twenty-one shillings. Because this was not an easy figure in which to calculate it was decided that the new unit piece should be worth twenty shillings. The size, fineness and weight of the sovereign were therefore adjusted accordingly. In due time, in the reign of George V, this piece and its half also passed out of circulation. The sovereigns now being struck at the Royal Mint are for technical and bullion purposes only.

As shown in the table above the largest silver piece was

again the crown. It was on this coin that Pistrucci's design of the St George and dragon, enclosed within the Garter, appeared at its best.

George IV suffered Pistrucci's caricature of his face for six years. He liked a bust of himself carved by Sir Francis Chantrey. Pistrucci was then ordered to copy this for the coinage. The artist, feeling it was beneath his dignity, refused. Various members of the famous Wyon family then largely took over coin design. The coinage of the short reign of William IV was also the work of a member of the Wyon family.

Agitation for a decimal coinage produced the florin or one-tenth of a pound, now known as two shillings. Originally put into circulation in 1849 without the letters D.G. (By the Grace of God) the first florins became known as 'Godless'. This was rectified in 1851. The introduction of the florin was the only concession made to decimalization at that time.

(*Top*) reverse, George I shilling; obverse, George I shilling; reverse, George II shilling. (*Bottom*) obverse and reverse of George II gold five guineas. The word 'Lima' on some coins of 1745-6 shows they were struck from bullion captured by Lord Anson in 1743 from a Spanish ship out of Acapulco.

Coins of George III and George IV. (*Top*) 'spade' type reverse of George III guinea; bust of George III by L. Pingo on the guinea; head of William Wyon on George IV halfcrown. (*Bottom*) George III crown; obverse and reverse of George III half sovereign.

The portrait on coinage produced to mark the Jubilee of Victoria in 1887 was derided and a redesign was made for the 1893 coinage, showing the Queen as a much older woman.

Meantime the pure copper coinage introduced under the Boulton and Watt contract in 1797 had proceeded through various designs. Now struck at the Royal Mint, some very fine Wyon-designed coins were produced. As time passed such pieces became too large and heavy and bronze was decided upon. This change produced the so-called 'bun penny'. The design by L. C. Wyon was the bronze penny at its best.

De Saulles, designer of the coinage of Edward VII, gave us one design of individual conception, the standing Britannia on the reverse of the florin. The design was well received, as was the artist's crowned shield of arms on the halfcrown and the lion-on-crown shilling. The coinage of George V was no more than a variation of previous designs. The crown almost 'died'

The superb design of St George and the dragon, by the Italian Pistrucci, on the reverse of the George III crown from 1818

but, reprieved in 1927, had only an inconspicuous reverse design. When Percy Metcalf produced a modernized form of Pistrucci's St George as the reverse design in 1935, this too suffered derision.

Much of the heraldic tradition in British coinage design continued into the reign of George VI. The crown was a fine piece, showing heraldry in all its majesty. A Scottish shilling was introduced as a compliment to the Queen consort and the twelve-sided threepence made its appearance. Drake's 'Golden Hind' appeared on the halfpenny and Britain's smallest bird, the wren, on the farthing.

In the present reign the heraldic 'mixture' has continued much as before. On the 1953 crown the Queen on horseback is a reversion to a design idea used in 1551. When Sir Winston Churchill appeared on the crowns of 1965 adverse comment was again heard.

Coinage metals

Over the centuries a large number of metals have been used for the purpose of striking coins. Certain Ancient Greek coins were made of electrum. A natural alloy of gold and silver, it has a white appearance. Electrum was found in a natural state but was later manufactured.

Gold has been associated with coinage ever since coins were evolved. Greece made use of gold for coinage from the beginning. From that time onwards gold has tended to be used for high value coinage.

The Roman Republic and Empire initially made little use of gold. Bronze and silver constituted the main coinage metals. It was not until the Empire that the Caesars ordained a gold coinage.

Gold coins reached Britain from the Continent with the successive waves of Belgic invaders. Ancient British coins copied from such pieces were in the main struck in gold.

The metal used for striking gold coins in Britain came from a variety of sources. At one time sufficient was found in Wales, Cornwall and the Cumberland area to make a significant contribution to the coinage. As the country expanded and coinage proliferated gold came from many sources. When a British prince married a foreign princess a dowry, frequently containing many gold coins, was often part of the marriage settlement. Usually the coins found their way to the mint for melting. Gold was obtained by way of ransom, by conquest and by looting in war. It was captured on the high seas in legitimate or piratical maritime action. As the trading companies began to push further afield to Africa and the Orient, gold was imported in the course of trade. Latterly supplies of gold had to be purchased, like any other commodity. It also has to be remembered that the coinage of past reigns is cannibalized at the mint.

Silver, as we have seen, served as a coinage metal from the remotest times. It reached Britain in much the same way as did gold. Reasonable quantities of it were mined in Wales. There was still sufficient in the reign of Charles I to cause Thomas

16th-century mining scene. The cut-down trees would have been used to provide pit-props, etc., and also charcoal for smelting ore.

Bushell to drain the mines of water and work them to a greater depth. He obtained sufficient quantities to make it worth opening a branch of the Tower mint at Aberystwyth Castle.

In the days when Spain ruled parts of Central and South America there seemed to be an inexhaustible supply of silver (and gold) available from that area, much of which reached Europe. Of this Britain had her share.

As coinage metals, copper and bronze are of equal antiquity with gold and silver. In Britain that thrifty Scot, James I (1603-25), saw a profit to be made from the granting of licences to strike small minor copper pieces. At the Restoration of Charles II (1660) the matter of a copper coinage received some better consideration, halfpennies and farthings being issued. By the reign of Queen Anne (1702-14), Sir Isaac Newton, then Master of the Mint, was experimenting with the metallurgical problems of a copper coinage. A well-struck and adequate issue did not really go into general circulation till 1797, when Boulton received his contract.

The rise in price of gold and silver, coupled with the

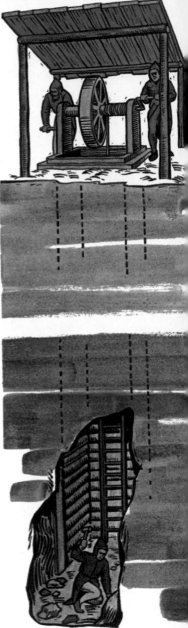

demand for increasing numbers of coins, has made it necessary to issue pieces of reasonably high face value in metals which have no relation to the stated value.

One of the first non-precious metals used to strike coins normally made in precious metal was nickel. The Chinese and the Bactrians had used an alloy of copper-nickel for coinage more than 2,000 years ago. Switzerland was the first of the modern countries to reintroduce nickel for coinage in about 1850. Various experiments were necessary in alloying nickel to produce a satisfactory coinage and a 75-25 cupro-nickel mixture eventually proved satisfactory. In Britain silver coins continued to be issued till 1946. The white coins after 1946 were struck in cupro-nickel.

Nearly all civilized countries are on the lookout for cheaper metals in which to produce their money. As a result many hitherto unknown for coinage are put into use. In Britain a shadow of the coming changes appeared in 1937 when the twelve-sided nickel-bronze threepence appeared.

Reverting to nickel and cupro-nickel, among other countries which occasionally issued pieces in the pure metal was Canada, with a five cent piece. The demands of World War II for this metal caused the Canadian piece to be struck in a substance known as tombac. This is an alloy of 88% copper and 12% zinc. Even tombac became scarce and the five cents was struck in chromium-plated steel.

During and after World War I in Germany almost any metal

Working down a German mine in the Middle Ages. Such scenes were shown on some German mining thalers.

was used for coins, iron being common. This and non-stainless steel soon rusted. The war reduced Germany to striking large numbers of token coins, again in various base metals. Among them were plated iron and zinc. Copper-plated zinc and copper-plated iron tokens were struck. Brass was used as a plating over a zinc or iron core. Iron was also enamelled and used for tokens.

As soon as it could be cheaply produced in commercial quantities aluminium offered itself as a white, non-rusting metal in which coins could be struck. As a rare metal, experiments in coining it were carried out before 1890. The Royal Mint was early in the aluminium coin field, since it issued one-tenth of a penny pieces in the metal for British West Africa in 1907 and 1908. In Brazil and the Belgian Congo, to mention but two countries, aluminium was alloyed with bronze to produce a coinage metal. Aluminium-magnesium was used for a time for coinage in French Oceania and Laos.

In 1965 the United States announced that it was striking its

(*Top*) tin coin from Siam; French chrome steel coin; Turkish coin of stainless steel. (*Centre*) copper-nickel coin. (*Bottom*) bronze half-penny; nickel coin; nickel-clad steel coin from Romania.

first coins in clad or sandwich metal. Sandwich metals, as opposed to plated metals, had been used for striking coins long before 1965. Afghanistan had coins in nickel-clad steel in the 1950s.

Boulton's proofs had a thick skin of gilt and withstood the heavy blow of the coining press. They therefore qualify for consideration as an early sandwich metal.

In the reign of George IV (1820-30), some proof pieces were struck in Barton's metal. This was a real clad or sandwich metal, having a copper core and a measurable thickness of gold or gilt on either side. It was never used for coins put into general circulation.

Charles Wiener, a Belgian coin and medal designer, made some models of his pattern sovereign of 1863 in cast iron.

Brass alone has not been much used for coinage though some pieces in this metal were struck for the Belgian Congo. Some copper-and-brass coins were struck for Afghanistan. Billon is a base metal usually made from a mixture of silver

(*Top*) Portuguese iron coin; nickel bronze piece from Yugoslavia; bronze Straits Settlements cent. (*Bottom*) Egyptian gold coin; Japanese tin coin; Hungarian aluminium coin.

A variety of shapes and metals:
1 copper, Ecuador; 2 zinc, Czecho-
slovakia; 3 aluminium bronze, Denmark; 4 zinc-coated steel, Belgium;
5 brass, Belgian Congo; 6 pure nickel,
Ireland; 7 silver, Canada; 8 brass-clad
steel, Germany; 9 nickel silver, China;
10 billon, Hungary; 11 nickel brass,
Pakistan; 12 copper nickel, Seychelles;
13 bronze, Morocco

and copper and we find coins struck from it in the Scottish series. Billon coins were struck for modern Hungary and for coins in Afghanistan in the early twentieth century.

Bronze-clad steel has been used for coins in Germany and stainless steel in Italy. Lead has appeared briefly, some Mexican coins having been struck in this metal in 1914. One more unusual metal, nickel-plated iron, has been used for coins in Poland.

Back in remote times Ancient British coins were cast in so-called tin. In fact the metal was speculum, a bronze core coated with tin. In the reign of Charles II and until the reign of William III tin halfpennies and farthings were struck in Britain. The coins usually had a copper plug inserted in the centre.

When the deposed king, James II, was fighting in Ireland with the hope of regaining the British throne, there was issued a large series of coins now known as 'Gun Money'. They seem to have been made of a mixture of brass cannon, bell metal, and almost anything else that came to hand.

Platinum is now a very rare metal and is classed with gold on this account. It was originally found in the Spanish gold mines of Darien but is also obtained from the Urals. This area being in Russia, some Russian coins were struck in platinum in the days of the Czars. Apart from some sets of proof coins, platinum is not much used for coinage in modern times.

Apart from metals pure and simple, and from the various objects mentioned in the chapter on 'curious currency', other substances have been used for coinage at various times.

It is held by some that coal, marked in some way, was at one time used for money, though this is somewhat doubtful.

In Siam, companies and traders at Bangkok issued tokens in porcelain from the mid-eighteenth century till 1871, when they were forbidden. The idea was revived in Germany after the Second World War, when series of porcelain pieces were made, many of them in attractive colours and even gilded. It is doubtful if these 'coins' ever circulated to any extent. It is also recorded that two English potteries adopted china or porcelain for token pieces. W. Davis of Worcester issued one and two shilling pieces, and John Coke produced five and seven shilling tokens in 1801.

In medieval times, punishment for forgery was savage. Here, a forger is about to have his hand chopped off.

They made their own money

A brief account should now be given of the forger and his work. Obviously, a coin forger is one who makes imitations of true coins and passes them into circulation. On the face of it one man, making a few of his own coins in a little back room, is not likely to create a financial panic. Where one such operator leads, however, others will follow and then the matter becomes really serious.

One of the underlying reasons why more and more effort has been directed towards the production of coins of a true weight, shape and fineness has been to render forgery more difficult. Once let forgery of money, either in coin or in bank note, get out of hand and a country can become flooded with worthless money and its economy undermined. Repercussions could well be felt in other countries as well.

The production of coinage has to be carefully limited. The whole picture has an air of artificiality, but it works. Just as the value of diamonds is held constant by restricting the number produced, so the value of money can be held constant in roughly the same way.

The rights of coining in any country have always been controlled and vested in the government. In ancient times death or mutilation – a hand or ear cut off – was the penalty for coin forgery. Now the penalty is a long prison sentence, with the confiscation of the coinage dies and the metal from which the coiner made his own money. It is one of those odd twists of history that, no sooner had Boulton and Watt fitted up the new Royal Mint with their machinery which could produce the most perfect coins so far issued in Britain, than a whole crop of forged coins of the second coinage of George III appeared. Such forgeries were made of silvered metals such as brass, copper, pewter and lead.

How does the forger go to work? It may be thought that the process of engraving and making coin dies is so difficult that few can attempt it. This is partly so, but where there is a will a way can be found. A man skilled in engraving metals for other purposes, such as jewellery-makers or glass-engravers, can easily divert his skill into copying coin dies. It can be readily understood, therefore, why such import-ance is placed on the custody of dies at a mint and in the honesty of those few persons who have access to them.

Two forgeries. The 'silver' coating has worn off, revealing the original coin metal beneath.

There are various methods by which forgeries can be made. Probably the most difficult, that of copying dies and finding a machine in which to strike coins from the dies, has already been mentioned. In the Far East some forgers work in a more simple way. From any given coin they produce a plaster mould. From this they cast a number of similar coins. Plaster is cheap enough and moulds can be made for a few pence. The coins so cast usually need a certain amount of touching up when they leave the mould, but in a less literate community their flaws are likely to go unobserved, and it is not difficult to pass them into circulation.

As a protection against such cast forgeries the British government introduced an edge marking, known as the security edge, on certain of the Commonwealth issues. To produce one coin from a plaster mould taken from a coin with this edge marking results in the mould having to be broken up after only one coin has been produced. Even then some plaster will be trapped in the grooves and markings of the security edge where it is difficult to remove.

In recent years a further method of forgery has been devised. It has been used to make valuable coins, such as forgeries of the British sovereign and rare coins of interest to collectors. The method entails the destruction of at least one such coin in order to make an impact die, from which further coins can then be struck. Purposely, no further details will be given of this expensive and complicated method.

The clipper is now mainly out of business. There are few coins left which are worth clipping. When coins were made of silver and gold by the hammer method, it was all too easy to clip or shave small amounts of metal from their irregular edges. Such clippings have been found. They look like the cuttings from finger-nails. Milled coins with either an edge legend or with grained edges did much to put the clipper out of business. Coins in valueless metal have completed the process. Even so it is on record that one genius invented a little machine that would cut the graining off a sovereign and at the same time cut a fresh graining. He worked in the days when sovereigns were in general circulation. It is understood that he worked in a bank, and that he was never actually caught using his ingenious device.

(*Right*) a plaster of paris mould used to forge Straits Settlements twenty-cent pieces. Illustrated reduced. (*Below*) Matthew Boulton, whose machinery made coins more difficult to forge, himself once surprised and broke up a gang of forgers at work.

Anything but coins

There are still a few groups of people who offer various articles in exchange for goods. Even though touched by the hand of civilization they are frequently against altering a method of exchange which has been customary to them for generations. The articles which primitive peoples use or have used for money are a theme of rich interest. Curious currency or, more light-heartedly 'funny money', is a study in itself.

In Africa the manilla was for centuries a popular and recognized form of currency. It took the form of a roughly horseshoe-shaped piece of metal, usually circular in section, with flattened ends. There are various accounts of the origin of the manilla. By some it is said that they were made from the metal bolts of ships wrecked on the African coast. Others are of the opinion that this form of currency came from ancient Egypt, or from the Phoenician or Carthaginian traders. Whatever the origin of the manilla, the Portuguese traders found it in use in the early sixteenth century.

There were about nine types of copper/bronze manillas in use in the Nigerian

(*Above*) aggry beads and West African manillas; copper cross from Katanga (not to scale)

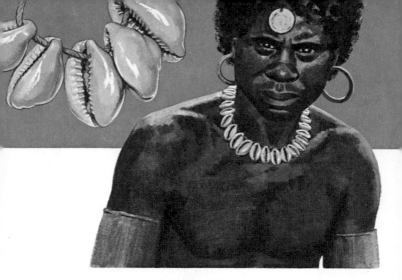

New Guinea native with cowrie shell necklace

area of Africa alone. They varied in size (up to about four inches across), and in weight, thickness and diameter. Each type was, however, instantly recognizable to natives of the country.

Manillas remained in circulation till 1948 when, in Nigeria, they were officially withdrawn. They also exist in silver, known as king and queen manillas. Finely wrought, these probably had no actual value, but just represented wealth. There are also varieties made of twisted metal, and coil manillas.

Sea shells are attractive, and make pleasant souvenirs. It was quite a normal reaction, then, that some of the fine shells found in hotter climates appealed to the native people and became a form of money. In particular the cowrie shell has been used for this purpose, over a very wide area. What is more interesting, perhaps, is that they became a form of currency even in parts of Africa where the cowrie shell is not found. Generally speaking, the smaller cowrie shells were those chosen for currency purposes. They were usually polished to bring out their attractive colouring and markings.

Some very large cowrie shells exist as currency, up to four

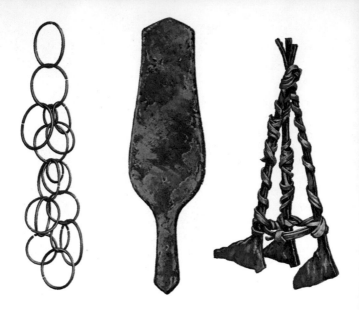

The objects on these pages (not drawn to scale) are forms of African currency. (*Above, left to right*) brass wire mitakos from the Congo; iron shoka from the Congo; iron fan axe money.

or five inches in length. It seems that these were used more among the islands of the South Seas than in Africa, where the value of the shell was independent of its size, the smaller being preferred by the shell merchants.

The cowries which found their way into the non-cowrie areas of Africa came mainly from round the Indian Ocean. In the mid-nineteenth century French and German trading companies were importing into Nigeria as many as 25,000 tons of Zanzibar cowries a year. The price paid on the West African coast was around £80 a ton.

The cowries of the Maldive Islands, where some of the inhabitants made a large part of their living by shell collecting, were distributed through centres in Bengal. Rates of exchange for the shells against the gold dinar seem to have varied widely between something like 400,000 and 1,200,000. From the Bengal trading bases they were sold at a considerable profit.

By the time they reached Nigeria the dinar bought some 1,150 cowries, while in London they cost around 1s 3d a thousand. In certain parts of Nigeria there was a rate of exchange between the larger and the smaller cowries, at the rate of two to one. Calculations varied in different parts of Nigeria, but the shells themselves were frequently equated as:

40 cowries = 1 string
50 strings = 1 head
10 heads = 1 bag (= 20,000 shells).

In spite of the above table the number of shells to a string could vary considerably. One very good reason why the cowrie shell formed such a popular medium of exchange was that it could not be forged or counterfeited.

In a world which rests for its survival on the products of the soil, it is logical that a certain value and respect was paid by primitive peoples to the implements with which the soil is tilled. It was but a step to such objects becoming items of barter and copies of them, often less than actual size, becoming a form of currency.

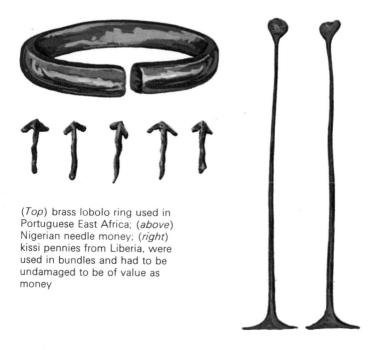

(*Top*) brass lobolo ring used in Portuguese East Africa; (*above*) Nigerian needle money; (*right*) kissi pennies from Liberia, were used in bundles and had to be undamaged to be of value as money

Chinese currencies. (*Top*) silver shoe money (sycee tael) and knife money; (*bottom*) bronze pu money and spade money.

In Ancient China spade-shaped pieces, known as Pu-money were known as far back as the Chou Dynasty (1122-255 BC). These pieces were originally flat, but later some had a hollow socket so that a piece of wood could be inserted and the piece carried in the hand. Such pieces were called Pu Spade-money. Many of the pieces have an inscription on them, frequently a town name, giving the money an origin and establishing its status.

A common form of Ancient Chinese curious currency was knife-money. This looks almost exactly like the blade of the so-called cut-throat razor. Like spade-money, it was usually of cast copper, bronze or possibly brass alloy. Around AD 7 a form of knife-money appeared which, to our eyes, looks very like the blank for a Yale-type door key. These pieces were inscribed with such legends as 'Ch'i knife five hundred' and 'One knife: value five thousand', the latter being inlaid with gold.

China also used another curious piece, known as bridge-money. Again cast, it had the rough appearance of the profile of a single-span bridge. Also from China the chop-marked dollar should be mentioned. This dollar could be a Chinese silver dollar-size coin or any other in the dollar series. As it passed from hand to hand among the merchants and bankers, each added his own chop mark, that is his own name or business house name, by stamping it into the flan with a punch.

The agricultural implement type of currency was a popular form of exchange in Africa. One of the most popular types was hoe money. This took various shapes, all more or less like a Dutch hoe. In Nigeria there were about ten named types. There were various ceremonial hoes, used as bride pieces or as a gift to the bride's father.

In some cases iron was used as currency in rough ingots, but pieces of various shapes and sizes were also used. There were Y-shaped pieces, spear-heads, fish-hooks and fish-shaped pieces, iron bracelets and long thin rods with T-shaped ends, known as Kissi Pennies. These were used in bundles and it is said that if they became damaged the spirit departed from the money and it was no longer accepted.

Copper and brass rods were also used, some of the latter bent

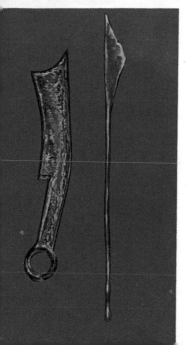

More Far East currencies. (*Left*) Chinese bronze knife money (chi tao) and chabili from Assam; (*top and centre*) Siam canoe money; (*bottom*) ticals (bullets) from Siam.

into U-shapes. In the late seventeenth century copper, imported in bar form, was split by the natives of Calabar into three parts, then twisted together and polished to make arm rings and similar objects.

Other curious African currencies included tobacco, mostly in chunks, twists or balls. Gin became an important currency. Bottles or whole crates went from hand to hand without ever being opened. One bottle could be worth five manillas.

Palm oil and cloth, the latter either in rolls or made into shirts and other articles of clothing have been used as currency, as have raffia fibre, yams, palm kernels, dried fish, feathers and groundnuts. Beads of glass, brass or stone were used as exchange media, as were axe-heads. These developed into various shapes for ceremonial purposes. Another form of weapon-money was the throwing knife. Some had a long handle and a semi-circular head ending in a bill.

Animals played their part as money. An interesting development was the bronze model of a cow or bull, mounted on wheels. Used in Borneo, this took the place of 'live' bride money. In the

Wampum (*left*), strings of beads fashioned from shells, was an early medium of exchange between settlers and American Indians

islands of the South Seas, classified as Oceania, we come across axe money again in New Guinea. Here also we find shells in various forms, some quite large, and tobacco sticks. From the same place come both natural and cultivated boar's tusk money, necklaces made of teeth, and beads and arm bands made of shells, as well as shell necklaces.

In New Ireland a particular type of red shell money was added to the shell currency. In the Marshall Islands plaited fibre belts were in use. In Borneo rattan was used as money, and in Santa Cruz feathers, perhaps the most fragile article ever to serve as currency. Red feathers were also used in parts of Nigeria. In Fiji whale's teeth, suitably strung, were a form of currency and in the Gilbert Islands Kekararo string. All these Oceania curious currencies were in use throughout the

Yap, in the South Pacific, can claim the world's heaviest money. Limestone 'coins' can be twelve feet across and weigh five tons.

eighteenth and the nineteenth centuries.

In the same period in China silver and gold 'boat' money appeared. An ingot of silver, varying in size according to value, was heated and then impressed with various stamps of ownership or origin. The impressing caused the edges of the silver to rise and the whole ingot, being rounded at the ends and tapering towards its base, took on the rough shape of a Chinese junk. Small gold ingots were similarly stamped.

In Siam and Malaya various interesting currencies appeared. Circular silver rods or bars of various sizes were cut into sections, heated, bent round till their ends touched and marked with the stamp of origin. Because of their shape such pieces became known as bullet-money. Gold bullet money was also in use at the same period, the nineteenth century.

Tin being available in quantity in this area it was natural enough that it should be used for various forms of currency. The Malaya tin tree-money is one of the most attractive forms. Molten tin was poured into a mould, filling an incuse design. When cool the tin came away in the shape of a large number of circular rings branching from the central spine, the whole object looking not unlike a tree. The rings could be broken off as and when needed.

In Siam at about the same period tin was used to produce what is now called hat-money. These pieces consisted of a square of tin. The centre of the square was raised into a four-sided, hollow, flat-topped protuberance. Various characters, the mark of origin or authenticity, were marked on the piece, which resembled a square hat.

In Africa, bracelets made of elephant tail hair were an eighteenth-nineteenth century form of currency. Such hair is not unlike wire strands and very strong. Modern tourists are sometimes sold plastic imitations of these hair bracelets. In West Africa miniature ornamented gun barrels were used as a medium of exchange. In Katanga large copper crosses about a foot across were used in the seventeenth and eighteenth centuries.

A form of currency common to parts of Russia and China is the tea brick. These are of the nineteenth and twentieth centuries, and may still be manufactured though not now used as money. Tea is dried and placed in a mould and subjected to heavy pressure. A thin brick, about $12 \times 6 \times 2$ inches is thus produced.

Iron bars and gold rings were both used as currencies in African countries

69

The Civil Wars of Charles I produced numerous siege pieces. (*Above*) a 1648 silver shilling from Pontefract and a Newark halfcrown, 1645.

Various designs are cut into the mould. Some bricks show the various stages in the making of tea bricks. Others have the Russian eagle, while others have a railway train. Many such bricks have been sent across Russia on the Trans-Siberian Railway.

Postage stamps have been encased in various ways and used as currency in many countries in the nineteenth and twentieth centuries. Municipalities throughout the civilized world have produced large quantities of tokens in various materials for use on trains, trams and omnibuses. Their inclusion here brings in the tin and other tokens still being issued by some shops as a rebate on prices paid, as well as the various trading stamps popular at the moment.

Such pieces are on the fringe of our subject. Not quite so much on the fringe are the large number of cut and counter-marked coins which have been used as money throughout almost the whole world. In Britain the Spanish eight reales was countermarked for use as legal tender. Private firms also countermarked such pieces for monetary use. In the West Indies a large number of such pieces were countermarked for local use in the islands. They were also cut into sections or had variously shaped pieces cut from their centres.

In Europe siege warfare gave rise to yet another form of curious currency, the siege piece or obsidional money. In Britain the Civil Wars of Charles I produced siege pieces at Carlisle, Scarborough, Pontefract, Newark and Colchester. These were mostly made from domestic silver objects. Irregu-larly shaped pieces were cut from such objects and stamped with a value usually equivalent to their weight.

Yet another form of curious currency is a series of what are generally called multiple thalers. The thaler, taler, dhaller, dollar, crown, five francs and piece of eight reales are all silver coins of about British crown size. A multiple thaler is thus an even larger silver coin with a denomination as large as, say, six thalers.

In some islands in the tropics where fishing is of prime importance, fish hooks attained an exchange value as currency. In the Dutch East Indies extraordinary pieces known as mokkos were in use until the nineteenth century.

Decimal coinage

It can be said with reasonable accuracy that, as far as coinage is concerned, the decimal system originated in the United States around 1792. By a law of 7 April 1795, France introduced a metric system of metrology and the franc was admitted into the coinage.

In Britain the need for an international decimal system of weights and measures was realized by James Watt, the engineer, as early as 1783. In 1819 a Commission set up to consider a system that included coinage as well, reported against the adoption of a decimal scale. Agitation continued not only in Britain but in the Empire and colonies. Australia, for example, had hoped for a decimal coinage in 1910 when its first series of coins was issued.

Patterns for a decimal coinage appeared early in Queen Victoria's reign. Finally the florin, a silver coin value two shillings or one-tenth of a pound, was introduced in 1849. Officially no halfcrowns were struck from 1850-74. Though the florin became accepted, it failed to produce further steps and halfcrowns began to be struck again in 1874.

Reverses of the decimal coinage of the United Kingdom, replacing the existing coinage after 15 February 1971

The 'Commonwealth Portrait' on Commonwealth decimal currencies

In the years after 1795 an increasing number of countries introduced a decimal coinage system. Economically the most powerful was the United States. Once independent of Europe in general and Britain in particular, North America (USA and Canada) settled on a dollar-based decimal system. Similar changes continued throughout the world until Britain, left almost alone among world powers, finally converted to decimal coinage on 15 February 1971. The first British decimal coins, the ten and five New Pence, equivalent to the existing florin and shilling, went into circulation in 1968. Several of the remaining smaller countries such as Ireland and the Fiji Islands, were also brought into the decimal system.

How much world trade and unification will benefit from a near-universal decimal coinage system only history can tell. There will still be differences in value between the various units of coinage in use. The next step, far ahead, would be the unification of all the decimal systems into a world-recognized coinage. But this comes too near to Utopia to be possible within foreseeable time.

Early Australian tokens. (*Left*) rare 1855 penny token issued by John Allen of Kiama; (*centre*) 1855 penny; (*right*) 1862 penny.

Australian coins

In this necessarily brief revue of coinage and its history no word has so far been said concerning the great influence which one country, Britain, had on the coinage of a large proportion of the world, the one-time British Empire which later developed into the British Commonwealth of Nations. A whole book, indeed a series of books could be, have been and are being written on this subject since the British Empire at its greatest extent gave rise to an almost incalculable number of coins which were issued in or for the many countries over which Britain once held sway.

In looking over the story of the many coinages which have been instituted for the numerous members of the British Empire and Commonwealth of Nations, one point at once stands out clearly. In almost every case no coinage was struck for any of the various territories gradually taken into the Empire till long after the need for a local coinage had caused hardship and financial loss in the country concerned.

This situation arose from a multitude of reasons too great to be dealt with here. An example can be taken from the coinage of Australia. Some countries which were placed under British rule, such as India, already had a currency. Others were trading with a miscellaneous selection of coins from many parts of the world which came into use as a result of trade with outside nations. South Africa and the West Indies are possible examples. In the sixteenth, seventeenth and eighteenth centuries it is reasonably true to say that the many countries with which the trading nations of Europe – Spain, the Low Countries and Britain – did business, accepted a selection of the coinages of these countries and drew up scales of equivalents between the various coins. The money of these great trading nations was trusted in the world at large.

But in the building of the British Empire currency was often a problem. Events in Australia show what can happen if sufficient supplies of coins are not available in a country being taken over or settled, either by the British or by any other country.

Magellan's followers are credited with sighting western Australia in 1522. It was not until 1770 and the coming of Captain James Cook that any real exploration of Australia took place. He stayed a week in Botany Bay while Sir Joseph Banks and Dr Solander collected thousands of species of flora.

Although the whole of the European trading world knew of Australia's existence, the first settlement there was made by the British at Port Jackson, now Sydney, in 1788. Further settlements followed. What was not, apparently, appreciated by the then British Government, was the fact that the settlers would set about building villages which grew into towns, and explore the interior of the great land mass in which they found themselves. This they did and, as always, money was needed to reward individual workers for their efforts.

It might be thought that English money would have gone into circulation, but in fact there was not enough to go round. As a result the majority of dealings had to be conducted by barter, as in the primitive times mentioned elsewhere. Rum, corn and other marketable produce was used, as was the Spanish eight reales piece (the Spanish dollar), that near-universal coin which, at one time or another during this period, was used in trade almost throughout the world.

The Spanish dollar arrived with the transports and other ships. For a time some ships' masters placed its value at 5s and others at 4s 6d, till the Governor proclaimed its value at 5s. Naturally, with such a variety of coinage in circulation, counterfeiting was not uncommon. Some idea of the miscellaneous money in use can be gained from a list published in 1800 giving their official exchange rates:

Guinea – £1 2s
Johanna – £4
Half Johanna – £2
Ducat – 9s 6d
Gold Mohur – £1 17s 6d
Pagoda – 8s
Spanish Dollar – 5s
Rupee – 2s 6d
Dutch Guilder – 2s
English shilling – 1s 1d
One ounce copper coin – 2d

In 1813 the Governor issued a proclamation which took the first step towards the introduction of a local Australian coinage. A quantity of Spanish dollars had been sent to help matters and it was ordered that a small circular piece should be cut from the centre and stamped with the words NEW SOUTH WALES below a crown on the one side and FIFTEEN PENCE on the reverse. The ring which remained was stamped on its inner rim with NEW SOUTH WALES 1813 on one side and FIVE SHILLINGS on the other. These pieces were known as dumps and holey dollars respectively. A few still exist, but they are now very rare collector's pieces.

Naturally they were soon counterfeited and as a result attempts were made to withdraw them. By 1828 the exchange value of the dump had fallen to 1s 1d, and of the holey dollar to 3s 3d. They finally went out of use in 1829.

Insufficient English money continued to be sent out and this was supplemented with Bank and private paper money. By

1849 tokens had begun to appear in Melbourne, and these quickly spread till each of the colonies which now make up Australia had token money in circulation. These continued in use till between 1863-8 when they were gradually demonetized. Some six hundred varieties were struck, a large number of them in Birmingham. If these pieces could be struck in Britain and successfully exported, why not the proper regal coinage?

Meantime another event occurred which only helped to make matters worse. Early in 1851 gold was discovered in New South Wales. There was a rush of 'diggers', but the results failed to reach expectations. Later in the year, in November, the Victorian gold fields at Mount Alexander were opened and by March of the next year, 1852, an estimated 8,000 males had left South Australia by sea, while hundreds of others made the journey overland. So serious was this exodus of the adult male population that it was only with difficulty that the harvest was gathered in. Since each 'digger' took with him as much ready money as he could, about two-thirds of the available coin was lost. Hardship fell on many. Prices fell. Heavy withdrawals were made on the banks and cash sales were almost unknown.

When the 'diggers' began to return around 1852, the general picture brightened somewhat as about £50,000 worth of gold arrived in South Australia with them. The scarcity of coin was at once felt, merchants and banks being forced to accept gold dust in payment for goods, at between 56s and 70s an ounce. As a result agitation again commenced for the establishment of a mint and the issue of sufficient coinage.

Officially though, the Governors of British Colonies were 'prohibited assenting in Her Majesty's name to . . . Any Bill affecting the Currency of the Colony'; though there was the proviso 'unless urgent necessity exists requiring that such be brought into immediate operation'. As Hunt Deacon wrote: 'Irrespective of the irregular communication between the mother country and Australia at the period under review, there can be no doubt that necessity did exist and as a consequence the first gold pieces struck for currency purposes in these colonies were those issued in South Australia under authority of the first Bullion Act of that Province, which it then was.' (Hunt Deacon, *The 'Ingots' and 'Assay Office Pieces' of South Australia*.)

The result, in 1852, was the appearance of thin gold pieces of irregular shape, roughly round or sometimes rectangular. These little gold plates were stamped with such legends as WEIGHT OF INGOT OZ. 0 DWT. 5 GR. 8 EQUIVT. WEIGHT OF 22 CARATS OZ. 0 DWT. 5 GRS 15/S.A./$\frac{1}{8}$/23/CARATS. These pieces, being 'unofficial' can be regarded as tokens, and are now of the greatest rarity.

The Government Assay Office was then empowered to issue gold tokens, and dies were prepared for £5 and £1 pieces. On the obverse they had the Imperial Crown in the centre with the date, 1852, below. The perimeter legend read GOVERNMENT ASSAY OFFICE ADELAIDE. In the centre of the reverse was the legend VALUE FIVE POUNDS, while the perimeter legend read WEIGHT. 1 OZ: 8 DWT: 4 GRS. 22 CARATS. The £1 piece was similar, with suitable alteration to the wording. No £5 pieces now appear to exist, save for some restrikes, and the £1 piece is very rare.

At last, in 1853, a mint was established in Sydney. A further mint followed in Melbourne in 1872 and another in Perth in 1899. Though these mints came closely under the control of the Australian government they were nominally branches of the Royal Mint in London and their work was summarized in the annual Report of the Deputy Master and Comptroller. Their primary object was that of coining sovereigns and half-sovereigns, based on the English type, in local gold, the master dies being supplied from London. These pieces carry the initial letter of the branch mint by way of a mint mark.

While all this was going on steam had begun to replace sail on the shipping routes of the world and the Suez Canal had been opened to traffic. Imperial coinage reached Australia in greater quantities. During the reign of Edward VII (1901-10) a separate coinage for Australia was at last put in hand. Florins, shillings, sixpences and threepences appeared in 1910 – no halfcrown was ever struck for Australia – but as this year was the last of the reign no very great numbers of Edward VII coins were struck.

Coin production was continued in earnest during the next reign, George V (1910-36), and the bronze penny and halfpenny were added. All the Australian pieces had their own individual designs. Imperial coinage was used concurrently with that of Australia till the early 1920s. Sydney mint closed in 1926 and Australia now had its own coinage produced in sufficient quantity to meet its needs.

In 1966 decimal coinage was instituted; in February 1965 a completely modern mint, the Royal Australian Mint, had been opened at Canberra, capable of producing 300,000,000 coins a year. Melbourne's Royal Mint stopped production in 1968 after 96 years.

In its struggle to exist and expand, Australia passed through many of the phases which we have seen in our account of the development of money in the world. Barter, primitive currency, tokens, the gradual emergence of a proper coinage – all are in the Australian coinage story. Australia, however, passed through all these stages of coinage development in something under 200 years.

(*Top*) Holey Dollar made from Charles IIII Spanish dollar; (*centre*) dump made from a Spanish dollar; (*bottom*) Adelaide gold ingot

FAMILY TREE OF BRITISH COINAGE
AFTER THE REFORM OF 1816

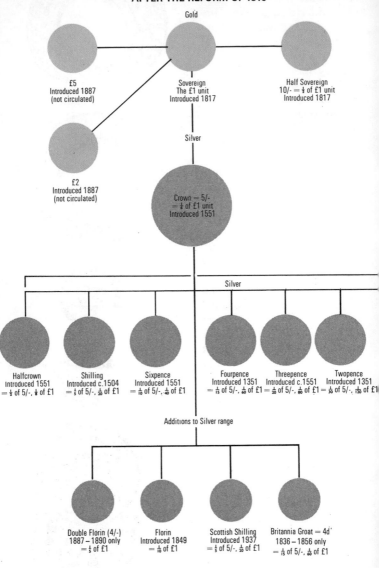

Gold

£5
Introduced 1887
(not circulated)

Sovereign
The £1 unit
Introduced 1817

Half Sovereign
10/- = ½ of £1 unit
Introduced 1817

£2
Introduced 1887
(not circulated)

Silver

Crown = 5/-
= ¼ of £1 unit
Introduced 1551

Silver

Halfcrown
Introduced 1551
= ½ of 5/-, ⅛ of £1

Shilling
Introduced c.1504
= ⅕ of 5/-, 1/20 of £1

Sixpence
Introduced 1551
= 1/10 of 5/-, 1/40 of £1

Fourpence
Introduced 1351
= 1/15 of 5/-, 1/60 of £1

Threepence
Introduced c.1551
= 1/20 of 5/-, 1/80 of £1

Twopence
Introduced 1351
= 1/30 of 5/-, 1/120 of £1

Additions to Silver range

Double Florin (4/-)
1887 – 1890 only
= ⅕ of £1

Florin
Introduced 1849
= 1/10 of £1

Scottish Shilling
Introduced 1937
= ⅕ of 5/-, 1/20 of £1

Britannia Groat = 4d
1836 – 1856 only
= 1/15 of 5/-, 1/60 of £1

Notes on the family tree of British coinage

English coinage did not really become British until 1707, when Scotland ceased to have a separate coinage.

The main reform of 1816 was the replacement of the guinea (twenty-one shillings) by the sovereign (twenty shillings), the thickness in each case being pro rata.

The £5 and £2 pieces, struck in proof only before 1887, had their origins in the five- and two-guinea pieces introduced in the coinage reform of 1662, in Charles II's reign.

Since 1946 all silver coins have been struck in cupro-nickel except the fourpence, threepence, twopence and penny which are now used only for the Royal Maundy money. After decimalization, the present Maundy money will continue to be struck, probably with a revised design.

Tin halfpennies and farthings were struck for a few years in the seventeenth century, but not since.

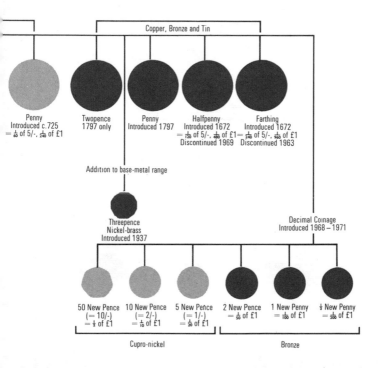

Copper, Bronze and Tin

Penny
Introduced c.725
= $\frac{1}{60}$ of 5/-, $\frac{1}{240}$ of £1

Twopence
1797 only

Penny
Introduced 1797

Halfpenny
Introduced 1672
= $\frac{1}{120}$ of 5/-, $\frac{1}{480}$ of £1
Discontinued 1969

Farthing
Introduced 1672
= $\frac{1}{240}$ of 5/-, $\frac{1}{960}$ of £1
Discontinued 1963

Addition to base-metal range

Threepence
Nickel-brass
Introduced 1937

Decimal Coinage
Introduced 1968 – 1971

50 New Pence
(= 10/-)
= $\frac{1}{2}$ of £1

10 New Pence
(= 2/-)
= $\frac{1}{10}$ of £1

5 New Pence
(= 1/-)
= $\frac{1}{20}$ of £1

2 New Pence
= $\frac{1}{50}$ of £1

1 New Penny
= $\frac{1}{100}$ of £1

$\frac{1}{2}$ New Penny
= $\frac{1}{200}$ of £1

Cupro-nickel

Bronze

Notes on the family tree of United States coins

The continental congress took the first steps towards a national currency in 1775, authorizing the issuance of bills on the faith of the united colonies. Before this, many of the colonies had issued their own coin and paper money in efforts to overcome the chronic money shortages which had bedevilled colonial finances from their beginnings.

One of the main tasks of the government of the new United States of America was to organize its finances and create a national currency. Robert Morris, superintendent of finance, began the planning of a mint in 1778.

It was his assistant, the US statesman and diplomat, Gouverneur Morris, who first put forward a plan for a new currency based on a decimal coinage ratio. This plan was included in Robert Morris's report to Congress in 1782. But Gouverneur

THE FAMILY TREE OF AMERICAN COINAGE REGULAR ISSUES

The chart on these and the following two pages traces regular coinage issues of the United States since 1793. The section on these pages is concerned with gold coinage.

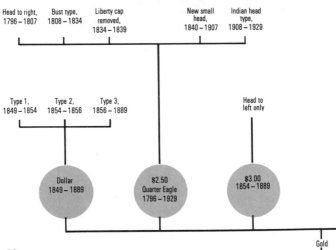

Morris's money unit was a complicated one, and in 1784 Thomas Jefferson proposed the simple dollar unit. This was a logical outcome of the fact that the Spanish dollar, or piece of eight, and its fractions, was the most widely used of the many foreign coins which had circulated in the colonies.

Congress approved the basic dollar unit in 1785, and in the following year agreed upon the coin denomination, the silver content of the dollar and the ratio of silver to gold. The Mint Act of 1792 established the national coinage and mint.

The first coins issued by the authority of the United States were the 1787 Fugio cents (*Fugio* = 'times flies,' the legend on the coins). These were copper coins, their reverse device of thirteen linked rings emphasizing the unity of the former colonies. The idea of having the president's head on coin obverses was rejected for mint issues as being monarchical.

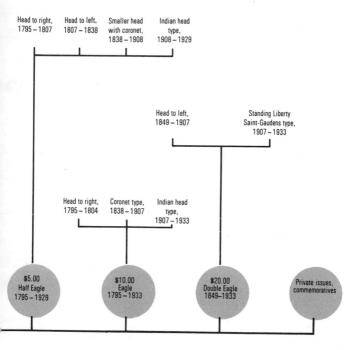

Continuing the United States coinage family tree, this section shows silver, copper and bronze coinage. The symbols used are: Ʀ—silver; Æ—copper or bronze; Æ-Ni—nickel-bronze; Ni—nickel.

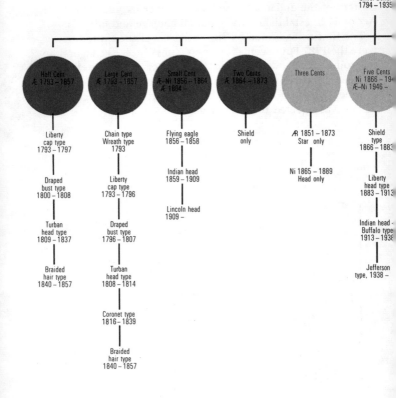

Silver Dollar
1794 – 1935

Half Cent Æ 1793 – 1857	Large Cent Æ 1793 – 1857	Small Cent Æ-Ni 1856 – 1864 Æ 1864 –	Two Cents Æ 1864 – 1873	Three Cents	Five Cents Ni 1866 – 19 Æ-Ni 1946 –
Liberty cap type 1793 – 1797	Chain type Wreath type 1793	Flying eagle 1856 – 1858	Shield only	Ʀ 1851 – 1873 Star only	Shield type 1866 – 1883
Draped bust type 1800 – 1808	Liberty cap type 1793 – 1796	Indian head 1859 – 1909		Ni 1865 – 1889 Head only	Liberty head type 1883 – 1913
Turban head type 1809 – 1837	Draped bust type 1796 – 1807	Lincoln head 1909 –			Indian head – Buffalo type 1913 – 1938
Braided hair type 1840 – 1857	Turban head type 1808 – 1814				Jefferson type, 1938 –
	Coronet type 1816 – 1839				
	Braided hair type 1840 – 1857				

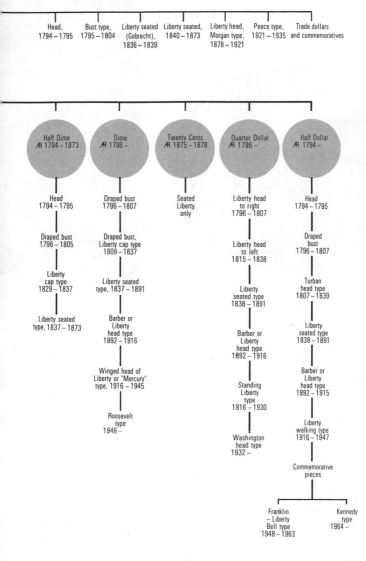

Head,
1794 – 1795

Bust type,
1795 – 1804

Liberty seated
(Gobrecht),
1836 – 1839

Liberty seated,
1840 – 1873

Liberty head,
Morgan type,
1878 – 1921

Peace type,
1921 – 1935

Trade dollars
and commemoratives

Half Dime
Æ 1794 – 1873

Dime
Æ 1796 –

Twenty Cents
Æ 1875 – 1878

Quarter Dollar
Æ 1796 –

Half Dollar
Æ 1794 –

Head
1794 – 1795

Draped bust
1796 – 1805

Liberty
cap type
1829 – 1837

Liberty seated
type, 1837 – 1873

Draped bust
1796 – 1807

Draped bust,
Liberty cap type
1809 – 1837

Liberty seated
type, 1837 – 1891

Barber or
Liberty
head type
1892 – 1916

Winged head of
Liberty or 'Mercury'
type, 1916 – 1945

Roosevelt
type
1946 –

Seated
Liberty
only

Liberty head
to right
1796 – 1807

Liberty head
to left
1815 – 1838

Liberty
seated type
1838 – 1891

Barber or
Liberty
head type
1892 – 1916

Standing
Liberty
type
1916 – 1930

Washington
head type
1932 –

Head
1794 – 1795

Draped
bust
1796 – 1807

Turban
head type
1807 – 1839

Liberty
seated type
1839 – 1891

Barber or
Liberty
head type
1892 – 1915

Liberty
walking type
1916 – 1947

Commemorative
pieces

Franklin
– Liberty
Bell type
1948 – 1963

Kennedy
type
1964 –

16th-century English coins. (*Right*) silver testoon, or shilling, of Henry VII; (*below*) 1551 silver crown of Edward VI (enlarged).

Collecting coins

Having seen something of how coins evolved and developed over many centuries we can turn our attention to those increasing numbers of people who collect coins. Collectors at this time fall, very broadly, into two classes, the scholar and the investor. The scholarly collector collects coins for a large number of reasons, but at base because some particular coin type, series of coins or background history behind a series attracts him. His first interest is not in the monetary value of his collection, though he appreciates that this will increase as his collection is built.

Probably foremost among the scholarly collectors is the increasing number specializing in the collection of Ancient Greek and Roman coins. The classical series has a collecting magic all its own. The history of Ancient Greece has become so mixed with myth and legend that one scarcely believes that such a State existed, until one reads some inspired history of Greece or, as more and more people are nowadays able to do,

Edward III silver groat

Scottish shilling, 1937

Edward VI threepence   1937 threepence

Reverse of the 1551 crown opposite

one visits Greece and sees its history at first hand.

Then the breath of life begins to re-enter the world of the Ancient Greeks. One begins to realize that they were men and women as we are, living in a highly civilized condition. Their facts and their legends are frequently illustrated in their coinage. Some Greek coins have a representation of the famous labyrinth in Crete. Such a story may well have had its origin in the claustrophobic tendencies deep-seated in so many human minds. In Greece the story passed into legend: in modern times it survives in, for example, the famous maze at Hampton Court Palace.

This gives some dim idea of the spark which inspires the collectors of Ancient Greek coins. Part of the Ancient Greek world lies in each individual piece. Its stories and its problems are written in metal. To a certain type of mind the attraction of Greek coins is irresistible, with its unanswered questions, its known facts and its references to the myths of the past.

Of the coinage of the Romans much the same can be said. Roman civilization throve for a time on conquest. As its influence expanded over Europe it brought with it the Roman monetary system. Very broadly, from the numismatic point of view the Roman civilization falls into two parts, the coinages of the Roman Republic and that of the Roman Empire. A third section, the coinage of the Eastern Roman Empire, is also relevant here.

The coins of the Roman Republic are of great academic interest; those of the Roman Empire are, perhaps, the more colourful. Once Roman Emperors came on the scene their heads began to appear on their coinage. As self-styled supermen of their age the Emperors were not infrequently promoted into god-figures.

Into the very middle of their world came the birth of Christ. That they looked upon Him as a trouble-making reformer is no more or as much discredit to them than is the discredit to us for having executed Thomas Moore, burned Joan of Arc or shot Martin Luther King.

The Romans, republican and empirical, built a world which in their day covered the majority of the known land. Their great buildings, their systems of water supply, their central heating, their roads and their towns can still be seen in various stages of decay. They left a mark on the world that can never be forgotten.

Here again the collector can make direct contact with the greatness of the past. With a few Roman coins in his hand the magic of collecting starts to work. He needs no academic education, there are books in plenty to assist him.

No less interesting are the coins of Europe, Britain and America. No less is the magic of the story that their study unfolds, of the scholarship that comes from their collection and study.

From all this one point may have appeared. The coinages of the world are so great in number, have been in existence so long and have so many sources of collector-interest that to try to form a time-wide, world-wide collection is usually out of the question. The collector must specialize along some line of interest which inspires him.

It matters not at all that when he starts collecting the

collector has no knowledge of the series of coins which, for one of a thousand reasons, sparks off his collecting interest. But, once started along the collecting road, his first consideration should be that of the condition. This is more important than rarity.

It can be said at once that coins taken from the money which passes from hand to hand in daily use are of little value to the collector. The embryo-scholarly collector soon begins to discriminate, to look around for coins of his own particular interest in the finest possible condition. Now let us take a look at his compatriot, the investor-collector.

The investor-collector has increased greatly as a product of the modern state of economic affairs. He has been brought into being by the proliferation of limited issues of pattern, proof and currency coins which have stemmed from the once innocent idea that a few collectors, *circa* 1830-1937, might like to buy a specimen set of proof coins offered by the Royal

(*From the top*) Elizabeth II 1953 Coronation cupro-nickel crown; Elizabeth I silver halfcrown; both sides of Victoria double florin

Mint to mark such occasions as the Jubilee of Queen Victoria, 1887 or the issue of the 'old head' coins in 1893.

When, after World War II, it was seen how such limited issues rocketed in value as an investment some of the older governments and most of the new states began to cash in on this source of revenue. Commemorative coins, limited issues of proof and currency pieces were but a logical development. In the main they have proved a good investment.

It is all too easy to say of the investor-collector that he has no real interest in numismatics but is out for a quick profit. But if one per cent of the investor-collectors turn into student-collectors, as indeed more than one per cent do, then the numismatic world benefits.

There are naturally various opinions concerning what is the most important consideration when collecting coins. Probably the condition of the coin is the greatest. As with any rule there are certain exceptions. Some coins are so rare that the collector must accept them in poor condition.

To help the collector, a series of symbols has long been in

United States coins. The Lincoln Head, shown (*left*) enlarged, first appeared on the US cent in 1909. (*Top, right*) obverse and reverse of the Indian head type half eagle. (*Below, right*) quarter eagle and gold three-dollar piece.

US coins. (*Top row*) obverse, Saint Gaudens type double eagle; 1796 half eagle; reverse of the double eagle. (*Centre*) gold dollar. (*Bottom*) 1794 silver dollar.

use by which the condition of a coin may be described. For a long time the letters FDC, standing for fleur-de-coin, were used to describe a coin in first class state. It is not really correct to equate FDC with the term Mint State. Strictly FDC not only describes a coin in the best possible condition in its series and for its age but in many cases the term pre-supposes a 'fleur', a bloom or patina, built up by years of careful human or accidental preservation.

The description Mint State or Uncirculated has now become widely adopted for use with modern machine-made coins. Such coins may not be absolutely perfect even if they are obtained direct from the mint itself. This is because coins intended for circulation are struck at high speed and then allowed to knock together while being checked, weighed and counted before being thrown into bags.

Below FDC, Mint State and Uncirculated, the next condition is Extremely Fine, abbreviated to EF. Here the coin has some slight wear or damage but not very much. Otherwise it would qualify for the description Very Fine, or VF. For a good collection this is about as poor a condition as is acceptable, save for the exceptions, mentioned above. In such cases, or on the ground of very high prices for a better specimen, coins in Fine (F) or Poor (P) condition may have to be accepted. Sometimes M is used for Mediocre, though its use has almost died out.

Not infrequently the condition symbols given above are qualified with the words 'about', 'almost' or 'nearly' in an honest attempt to give as true a description as possible. Sometimes the symbols are written VF/EF, usually meaning that the coin is better than VF but not quite EF.

The symbols are also sometimes written EF-VF, usually meaning that the obverse, or 'head' side of the coin is EF

US coins. (*Top to bottom*) silver dollar; quarter dollar, first issued in 1796; quarter dollar with Washington head; Liberty Bell half dollar; Liberty seated half dollar.

while the reverse, or 'tail' side is VF. Save in very special cases a coin that has been mounted for use as an ornament or which has had a hole drilled through it is quite worthless as a collector's piece.

Next in importance to condition is rarity. If you can afford it, collect rare coins. They will be expensive and the value of a collection of such pieces appreciates considerably. They will not necessarily give the collector any more satisfaction than will a well-built collection of more common pieces if, as is so often the case, the purpose of collecting is the pleasure of forming the collection and the interest and knowledge which its formation brings.

To describe the metal of which coins are made, AV = gold, AR = silver, AE = copper or bronze. Recent metallic developments have added Ni = nickel, Cu-Ni = cupronickel. Lead, brass, tin, pewter or platinum or any of the less common metals are usually written out in full. Pl. was

US coins: half dollar reverse, 1916-47; obverse and reverse of 1827 large cent; 1859 small cent; reverse of 1804 dollar, 1st type

The double eagle ($20 gold piece), the reverse of which is here illustrated enlarged, was the largest of all US regular issues

once used for lead, but has now almost dropped out of use.

The collector of coins must specialize. The number of possibilities is endless. The following list indicates very broadly some possible themes:

Coins of a state or country
    of a particular period of a state or country
    of one of more rulers of a state or country
    of one method of manufacture (hammered, milled, etc.)
    of one particular metal (gold, silver, nickel, etc.)
    of a particular design (coat of arms, ships)
    of one or more denomination (crowns, pennies, etc.)
    of a country or series of countries no longer in the same political existence, such as the German states, the British Empire, the coins struck by one country when in occupation of another for use in the occupied country
    of a religious interest, showing deities: or used for some religious ceremony like Maundy money and Touch pieces

showing views of towns in times past: the European series
very rich in such pieces

showing industrial scenes or machinery, such as mining
Talers

Specimen sets

New issues

Curious currency

Siege pieces and emergency money

Trader's tokens

Pattern and proof coins

Commemorative coins, struck to mark some event

Commemorative medals, struck for the same purpose

War medals and civil and military decorations

Countermarked and cut coins, such as West Indian

Even within such headings there are still possible divisions
into more specialized themes.

With all these possibilities before him the new collector is
well advised to start on one small theme and then expand his

US coins: (*top*) Liberty head type dime; 1806 quarter eagle;
reverse of five-cent piece, 1866-83, 2nd type. (*Centre*) reverse of
Liberty head dime; 1824 dime; buffalo reverse on five-cent piece;
1797 half cent. (*Bottom*) obverse and reverse of the Oregon Trail
Memorial coin; large cent, 1796.

collection over the years as other interests appear. If money is no object one can collect omnivorously and enjoy it. But if every penny has to be considered before it is spent perhaps even greater satisfaction is obtained as the collection grows and one more desired piece is added to it.

Enough has now been said to give a general indication of some of the basic rules of coin collecting. We might now look a little further into one or two collecting themes.

To many collectors the crown/dollar/thaler-size piece offers many attractions. It is usually the largest coin in a series of silver/cupro-nickel pieces and thus stands at the head of a line of smaller denominations. It is large enough to allow the coin engraver the maximum scope for his art. It therefore usually contains a fine contemporary portrait on the obverse and an interesting design on the reverse. As a denominational size it exists in profusion on a global basis.

While it is not suggested that a collector should try to specialize in the crown-size coins of the world, which are once again an immense subject, there is a great field of specialization in this one coin-type, and various sub-collecting themes, based on some of the dollar-size pieces offer themselves as an objective.

From one such angle, the collector may specialize in the crown-size pieces of one particular country or state. Having got together a reasonable collection he can then expand by taking in the smaller denominations, the 'family' of the crown piece. In Britain this would mean adding halfcrowns, florins (after 1849), shillings and sixpences. Each of these smaller pieces is also a collecting theme in itself.

Let us take a look at another, the Spanish eight reales piece, already briefly mentioned. This is a crown-size piece in silver. It begins to appear with the Spanish conquests on the American continents and their exploitation to the limits of all the gold and silver to be found in their conquered land. Their influence in the area was strongest from the fifteenth to the eighteenth centuries.

Once the vast store of metal had started to be worked the question arose of how to deal with it. The silver was cast into bars and in the early stages pieces of metal were cut from the bars and struck into roughly-shaped eight reale coins. Mints

Four Spanish eight reales pieces (the Spanish dollar) of the kind used in pre-Independence America and in Australia

were set up in America, as at Mexico, Lima and Potosi.

The eight reales pieces were produced in millions. They became recognized among the traders throughout almost the whole world. The merchants of Britain, Holland and Portugal, to name but three, used them in their original state and they were accepted as far away as Malaya and China.

They were purchased in quantity by the British government during a period of coin shortage in the reign of George III. First countermarked, they were later planed flat and then restruck as Bank of England (and Bank of Ireland) dollars. They were restruck as coins for Madras, as Straits Settlements dollars as late as the reign of Edward VII, were cut and countermarked for the islands of the West Indies. What fields for specialized collecting this one romantic coin offers. Its story reveals just one facet of the interest of coin collecting.

Where to obtain coins

The various sources of supply open to the coin collector now need some explanation. Though many a collector has started by putting aside a few coins from the money in his pocket, this source of supply soon becomes inadequate and rarely yields coins which are worth retaining in a collection. Such pieces are usually already worn. It is as good a start for coin collecting as any, but the collector must soon look around for other sources of supply.

Broadly these sources are through the established coin dealers, by purchase at coin auction sales, by purchase from general antique dealers who may have coins pass through their hands, and by miscellaneous means. Let us consider these sources of supply in that order.

Throughout the world there is a large number of established coin dealers. They specialize in this one subject, coins for collectors. Some of them are old-established firms, though as the interest in coin collecting grows daily, more and more dealers come into the field. Many of the smaller dealers buy at a discount from the larger dealers and a general internal trade is thus carried on.

The collector can find the established dealer in various ways, mainly through advertisements in the daily press and the many specialized numismatic journals of the world. Many of the larger dealers publish their own coin magazines and price lists, such as Spink's *Numismatic Circular*, Seaby's *Coin and*

Medal Bulletin, Corbitt and Hunter's *Numismatic Gazette* (all British), and Coin Galleries' *Numismatic Review and Fixed Price List* (USA).

The primary function of the coin dealer is to supply the collector with coins. To this end he deals with the collector on a personal basis. He studies his customer, advises him in every possible way on all facets of coin collecting and, knowing the wants of each of his customers, offers them suitable coins when they are available. The dealer will also buy from the collector, as well as from the non-collector who may have coins which are of interest or value. If a collector changes his collecting theme the dealer will buy the coins which no longer interest the collector and find for him coins of his new interest. In the rare event of a collector giving up collecting altogether the dealer will often buy the whole collection for cash, or sell it on commission over a period.

Most of the larger coin dealers trade in the coins of the whole world and with the coins of every period of time. Naturally, emphasis is laid on the coins of the country in which the dealer is established. Some of the more recently established

Scene at a typical coin auction

dealers, many of whom have been brought into business by the healthy and increasing interest in modern coins, confine their interests to these issues.

The collector may therefore put his trust in the established dealer, who has a reputation to uphold. In any form of trade nothing is so fragile as the trader's reputation. Only by scrupulous care of it can the dealer hold his business and his customers together.

The dealer serves his customer in many other ways. He usually attends auction sales of coins in person, bidding for coins for stock and for those of his customers who give him commissions. He will also advise on the possible price of any lot and will secure it as much below his customer's commission price as the opposition in the sale room will permit. On the other hand there is no reason at all why a collector should not attend auction sales in person and have all the thrill of bidding for himself.

Two important facts concerning buying at auction in Britain should be mentioned. Most of the larger British dealers charge their customers only five per cent commission on the total amount spent by the collector on lots bought at the sale on the collector's behalf. Secondly, in Britain there is no sales tax on works of art, including coins, which are sold by auction. This is the real key to the fact that Britain has long been the centre of the art auction world.

Coins, both individual pieces and whole collections, reach the auction room by various routes. A collector may, by direct approach, instruct a coin auctioneer to sell his collection, or he may put it in the hands of his dealer with instructions to sell at auction. The auctioneer may have a coin expert on his staff who will catalogue the collection to its best advantage. The auctioneer may retain the services of one of the larger dealers who will catalogue coins for him. In either case the collection will be offered in the most advantageous form. It should be pointed out that the auctioneer's commission for selling a collection is about 12-15 per cent or more. It is not related to the small commission which a dealer will charge for *buying* coins for a collector at an auction sale.

The general antique dealer, who is next on our list of possible sources of supply, may well have a few coins on hand.

He may not know a great deal about them, and it is therefore sometimes possible for the coin collector to obtain a bargain. With the proliferation of coin catalogues showing approximate valuations such chances become increasingly rare. So also does the chance of being greatly over-charged for a coin by an antique dealer who, having no knowledge of coin values, plays safe by asking a high price.

Other ways of obtaining coins include auctions organized by local coin clubs or societies, and private exchanges arranged between their members.

In recent years the growing interest in coin collecting has also generated a number of coin fairs. These help to promote and popularize collecting, by enabling the dealer to come out and meet the general public and attract their interest.

Displays in the Modern Coin Department of a large numismatic dealer

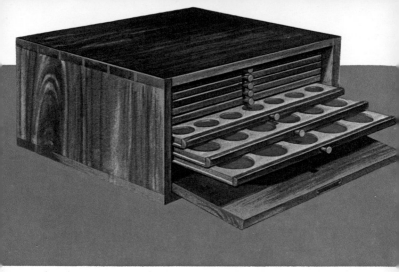

A mahogany coin cabinet, though expensive, is the best means of housing a valuable coin collection

Caring for and displaying the collection

A coin collection has cost money to build, and it should be looked after with the greatest care. The best method of keeping a coin collection is to house it in a proper coin cabinet. Cabinets vary in size and consist of a number of thin trays running in grooves, each tray pierced with circular holes, each hole taking one coin. Various sizes of holes are necessary for a general collection. For a specialized collection of one type of coin all the trays may be pierced with holes of the same diameter. A smaller hole cut through the base of the main piercing allows the coin to be raised from below rather than lifted out from above, an action which sometimes allows a finger-nail to scratch the surface of the coin. A piece of thin dry cloth, such as billiard-table felt, usually lines the base of each piercing. Cabinets should be made of well-seasoned mahogany, thus eliminating dampness in the wood itself which can tarnish coins.

Coin cabinets can be obtained new or second-hand. In the former case they can be built to suit the requirements of the individual collector. Though not over-priced they are reasonably expensive and are a pleasing piece of furniture. The smaller cabinets are portable and can be locked in a safe during any prolonged absence of the collector. They are usually provided with double locking doors.

When buying a cabinet considerable thought should be given to the ultimate size of the collection and to the sizes of its individual pieces. A small coin will fit into a large piercing, though wasting expensive space. A large coin will not fit into a piercing smaller than itself. Most cabinets are fitted with trays pierced with about four basic-size holes for crowns, halfcrowns and florins, shillings and sixpences. Custom-built cabinets can be fitted with any arrangement of piercings and, if needed, with a flat open tray. Naturally the trays should be interchangeable in position within the cabinet. If more than one cabinet is required the trays should be interchangeable between them. Coin cabinets have been made of metal and man-made plastic materials but for various reasons they are not usually as satisfactory as those made of mahogany.

Coin albums in book-form, fitted with pages of transparent plastic, each page containing coin-pockets, are now a popular and inexpensive method of housing a coin collection. So far as is known, such plastic material does not damage a coin or cause it to tarnish. But, since it is absolutely unabsorbent in certain circumstances, condensation can take place within the pocket and thus tarnish the coin. As a general rule coins should not be kept in such a humid atmosphere as to allow this condensation to occur.

A plastic coin album allows both sides of a coin to be seen readily

When buying such a coin album points to look for are the strength of the page at the hinge and the strength of the cover. Coins are heavy and a well-filled page may break away at the roots. An advantage of an album is that it allows both sides of the coins easily to be seen. Some collectors write details of the coins on slips of card and insert them in the pocket next below the coin in question.

Coins should never be kept wrapped up in any form of paper or in household envelopes for any long period. Such paper has a high water content and printing ink is capable of tarnishing coins. Special coin envelopes of dry paper are available from coin accessory dealers and should be used by the collector who wishes to keep his coins in this way. The disadvantages of this, the cheapest method of housing coins, is that they cannot readily be seen, though their details can be written on the envelope itself. The methodical collector will include the price paid for each specimen, usually noted in a private code. This enables him to see what he has spent and how his coins may be appreciating in value. It also allows him to take total now and again and increase the insurance of his collection as necessary. Many coin dealers can arrange for the

Plastic envelope for single coins and a coin holder, generally used for sets or types of coins

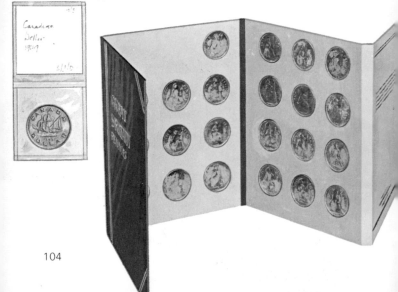

insurance of coin collections through their own brokers.

Collectors of type-sets of coins, such as British shillings, pennies or threepences, are now provided with folding card holders. These are pierced with holes to take each coin and the date of the coin is printed below. These folders are excellent for this type of collection. Once again, they should be scrutinized for the possible water content of the materials from which they are made and for their strength to carry their load of coins.

Coins may be dirty or tarnished when the collector obtains them. He may wish to clean them in order to appreciate them to their best advantage. The cleaning of coins needs care as any rough treatment will scratch and damage them.

With gold and silver coins a preliminary cleaning can be carried out by simply washing the coins in soft soap and water, drying them thoroughly afterwards. In theory gold coins can be cleaned with acid. All gold coins have a greater or less amount of alloy in them and this the acid will attack. A weak acid such as lemon juice is therefore recommended.

Silver coins can be cleaned with household ammonia and a piece of jeweller's cotton wool. In both cases the coin can be

Envelopes of special dry paper are an inexpensive way of storing coins

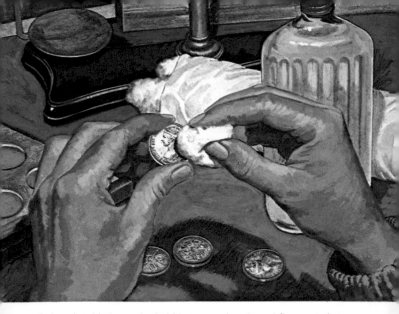

Coins should always be held between thumb and finger so that only the edge is touched

gently brushed afterwards with a soft silver-brush. In cases of mild tarnish simply breathing on the coin and then brushing it will frequently bring up a pleasing tone. The softness of the brush is all-important. None of these cleaning methods should be used for pattern or proof coins.

In general, domestic silver polishes should not be used to clean silver coins. Some of them leave a white deposit in the smaller parts of the design. Methylated spirit is another gentle cleaning agent which, like ammonia, evaporates leaving the coin dry.

As a general rule copper and bronze coins should not be cleaned. Attempts to clean may result in verdigris and this is almost impossible to remove once it starts to form. A light breath and a little soft brushing will often bring out the tone and patina on a bronze coin, but it is not recommended that an amateur try anything more than this without expert advice.

Nickel and cupro-nickel coins do not tarnish in quite the same way as silver. The metal is harder and will stand slightly more vigorous cleaning. But as with any cleaning method, care must be taken so that the plain surfaces do not become scratched. The few tin coins which the collector may encounter are frequently corroded. It is not recommended that any attempt to clean them be made without expert advice. Aluminium coins in theory stay bright, but in a hot damp climate certain coins of alloyed aluminium can become very corroded.

Coins should always be handled by their edges. It is wrong to rub one's finger over them. The slight dampness of the human hand can cause tarnish to start on silver coins and can damage copper and bronze. Coins held by their edges between the thumb and finger will suffer no damage. Tempting though it may seem when a collector has filled one cabinet or album, two coins should not be put together in one piercing or album pocket.

Reference was made to pattern and proof coins as needing special treatment. It would be well to explain what pattern and proof coins are.

Broadly speaking, a pattern piece is one struck from a design which is not afterwards used for a coin put into general circulation. The dies from which they are struck are polished

Gentle cleaning with a
soft silver brush will
not harm coins

before use, as are the blanks of the coins. The result is a coin with a mirror-like finish, the design complete in every minute detail. Such pieces are struck one at a time and removed from the machine by hand.

Proof coins are produced in the same way. They are proof pieces of coins which will go into circulation. When a new coinage is designed for a country it is frequently struck in proof form so that all concerned are satisfied with the final result. From the striking of the proof coins for official purposes has sprung over the past 150 years the custom of offering sets to the general public when a new coinage is introduced.

Obviously such sets, usually offered in fitted cases of velvet and plush, are sold at prices above the face value of the actual coins. Commercialization of the limited proof set idea has led to proliferation. Similar issues have become a source of revenue for many of the newly-born countries and a source of investment for one type of investor-collector.

Various occasions arise when coins need to be exhibited. In British numismatic societies and clubs it has long been the custom for collectors to pass round for members to view coins which have some bearing on the lecture normally given by the speaker of the evening. Members know enough about coins not to treat such exhibits in the wrong way. This is exhibiting coins in the most simple way. It makes no pretence of glamorizing the exhibit.

In America exhibitions of coins at club meetings frequently take a different form. Various collectors stage thematic exhibitions, which may or may not have direct reference to any lecture that may be given. A collector of Victorian crown pieces would probably lay out a showcase illustrating the various types, possibly with a picture of Queen Victoria as a centre piece. Captions would explain the various types issued. At the same meeting members would offer as exhibits cases or layouts of many other coins.

Such thematic exhibitions are frequently carefully and strictly judged by a panel. They would be considered under such headings as the completeness of the exhibit, the condition of the coins shown, the correctness of the information given and the eye-appeal of the exhibit.

Coins themselves are not easy objects to exhibit in an appeal-

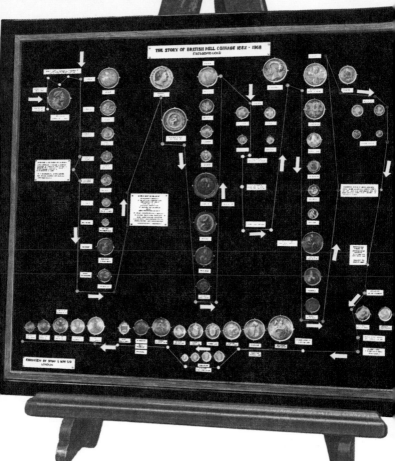

This fine coin display tells the story of British milled coinage, 1662-1968, excluding gold. The frame is 27ins. × 24ins.

ing way. Single specimens passed round, while of interest in themselves, leave it to the knowledge of the observer to fill in the background. Thematic exhibitions often need some background, such as pictures or maps, to assist them in telling their story.

As an example, the Midland Bank Limited has a travelling

exhibition showing the history of British coinage from Elizabeth I to Elizabeth II. The coins of each reign are displayed below the portrait of the king or queen in whose reign they were issued. Various visual aids add colour, such as a picture of a sea battle to help explain the word LIMA on some of the coins of George II, a picture of Queen Elizabeth II distributing Maundy Money to explain this ancient custom, or a picture of coins being struck at the Royal Mint to show how modern pieces are actually made.

Let us suppose a collector is preparing to arrange an exhibition on our old theme the British crown piece. Postcard pictures of the contemporary portraits of the various kings and queens can be obtained from the National Portrait Gallery. Illustrations of what some part of Britain looked like in any particular past age can be obtained from such sources as the Print Room at the British Museum. Outline maps to show, for example, the branch mints operating during the reign of William III can easily be drawn from an atlas. Travel brochures, newspaper colour supplements, picture libraries, the commercial photographic agencies and government information offices are all rich sources for pictures of all kinds.

Having assembled his material the collector now lays it out in some form of showcase. A fairly large converted picture frame suggests itself, though depth from front to back may have to be added. The coins must be held in position in the various groups decided upon by the exhibitor.

It need hardly be said that the coins should not be held down on the backboard with some form of adhesive, or that the backboard should be covered with a piece of velvet, felt or dry cloth. Three ordinary short household pins will retain a coin in position and a backboard of soft wood will allow the pins to be driven in by hand.

Captions and long explanations look quite presentable if typed on a piece of thin card. Pieces of gold or coloured thread, or the little red paper arrows used by the philatelist, can be added to direct the observer's eye.

The preparation of such exhibitions can add much to the collector's interest. Perhaps what little has been said will sow a few thoughts which may germinate in a way that brings coin collecting more to the notice of collector and public.

Bullion seized from Spain in Vigo Bay found its way into the Queen Anne coinage

ANNA DEI GRATIA

VIGO

The John Sanford Saltus Medal of the British Numismatic Society

Coin societies and clubs

Among the ever-increasing number of coin societies in Britain, the Royal Numismatic Society, founded as the Numismatic Society of London in 1836, is the oldest and the senior. It ranks among the learned societies of the country and meets at Burlington House, Piccadilly. The President, always a numismatist of eminence, presides over the monthly meeting of fellows. Its transactions are published annually in the *Numismatic Chronicle,* together with the President's annual Address, reviews of important new books and writings, and a list of Fellows.

By the end of the nineteenth century, it was felt that more consideration should be given to British numismatic subjects and the British Numismatic Society was founded in 1903. This society concerns itself in the main with the 2,000-year-long subject of British numismatics. Its meetings are held each month at the Warburg Institute in the heart of the University of London and its transactions are published annually in the *British Numismatic Journal.*

The Royal Numismatic Society's gold medal

Both the Royal and the British have libraries of world importance, containing books, pamphlets and papers on every phase of numismatics. Both libraries are housed in the Warburg Institute and Fellows and Members have free use of them.

With nearly fifty provincial societies affiliated to the British Association of Numismatic Societies and an unknown number not affiliated, it is fairly safe to say that there is a society within reach of practically everybody in the United Kingdom. Most of the societies and clubs meet about once a month. The usual course of events at meetings is for a member or a visiting speaker to give a short lecture, usually embellished with exhibits and frequently with slides. A few societies publish their transactions, thus recording their contribution to numismatics as a whole.

Most towns in which societies are formed have a museum, which may or may not have a collection of coins. On the face of it the local museum would appear to be a most suitable place for a coin society to meet and this kind of association is increasingly coming into recognition. Some museums now

The American Numismatic
Society, New York

welcome the local numismatic society and encourage its members to meet in the museum. An example of how a museum and local societies can work together is to be found in Bournemouth, England; but it is only given as an example. There will be other museums which go even further, though none with more genuine purpose.

This popular seaside town already possesses the Russell-Cotes Art Gallery and Museum, now administered by the local education committee. Under the enthusiasm of the present Director, Graham Teasdill, Fellow of the Royal Numismatic Society, a transport historian and a connoisseur of art forms in general, the local numismatic society was at once invited to hold its meetings in one of the Gallery's fine rooms.

The interest of the children in the contents of the gallery as a whole was encouraged. A Children's Club, meeting once a week, was instituted. The Club elects its own president, secretary and committee, and study sessions are held, at which the Director frequently gives an informal talk. Informality is encouraged as far as possible and is an essential oil in the smooth turning of the wheels of education. The Director's subject may be any of his many interests. If the subject is coins, examples are passed round for the children to see and handle, and for them to make their own rubbings.

Since the local numismatic society meets once a month in the museum later in the evening, the speaker not infrequently gives a talk to the Children's Club before his more serious lecture to the Wessex Numismatic Society later in the evening. Thus a link is forged early in life between the children who are interested in coins and the local numismatic society, which they may join as junior members.

Apart from these activities the museum provides an extra-mural service to the local schools. This includes the reception of school parties to see the museum's collection of coins; lectures are also given in the schools on the story of money, illustrated with film strips and slides and backed by a tape-recorded commentary. Coins and electrotype copies of rare coins are also passed round. The children are encouraged to answer a simple questionnaire on the subject of the lecture.

This is just one example of how a local museum offering facilities to the local numismatic interest can foster coin collecting. The great national museums in any country offer much to the student. The local museums can add the personal touch, in numismatics as in any other subject.

Superbly planned coin displays at the American Numismatic Society

Collections in museums

The world's finest coin collection is in the British Museum, London. While other museums have more specialized collections and thus may be richer in one or more particular field of coins, the British Museum collection for its breadth, depth and overall coverage is acknowledged by those competent to voice such opinions as the finest. It is housed behind locked doors, steel gates and heavy security. Since coins are best studied by the showing of individual pieces and by the exhibition of an open coin tray filled with specimens, the strict surveillance by the staff of the visitor to the Department is absolutely essential.

At present the British Museum makes small attempt so to display its great numismatic wealth. This is through no fault of the Keeper of the Department, but is the long shadow of the war damage which fell on the museum between 1939 and 1945. To the numismatic student, the honest enthusiast and the earnest inquirer the treasures of the collection will gladly be shown. Quite unexpected facilities are available. Coins may be studied *in extenso,* photographed, artists may make drawings of them, plaster casts of specimens can be provided. A bank of such casts is available.

Second only to the great collection itself is one of the world's finest and most complete libraries of numismatic works. The contents of this library are also open to the student. Inquiries by letter, telephone and personal visit, pour into the department in a never-ending stream.

Nor is the collection finalized and finished. The Museum adds to it yearly by direct purchase, accepts gifts from collectors and receives the outcome of 'treasure trove', for which it pays the market value. To the staff the collection must appear like the results of the activities of the 'Sorcerer's Apprentice'. No sooner does it appear that the final cataloguing of any particular series of coins is in sight of completion than fresh material arrives.

Let not all this inhibit the serious student and collector from visiting the collection. It is public property and there for the public to see. Given the necessary security precautions, the

(*Left*) Coin and Medal Department of the British Museum, London

The Heberden Coin Room, Ashmolean, Oxford

sifting by the staff of the frivolous from the serious enquiry and the collection is freely and gladly exhibited.

Runners-up in Britain for the title of the world's finest collection of coins are those of the Ashmolean Museum, Oxford and the Fitzwilliam Museum, Cambridge. Here the picture is different. Both collections are the property of their respective museums. Again these collections are neither finalized nor finished. Purchases are made from among the coins offered by private and public sale and donations are received every year.

At the Ashmolean, the Heberden Coin Room is able to put on permanent exhibition a considerable number of coins. Here again there are working facilities for the student and casts, slides and photographs can be supplied. There is also a fine library of numismatic works.

In Cambridge the Fitzwilliam Museum coin department has a homely feel about it. Again the collection as a whole is probably beyond price. Perhaps the homely feeling is derived from the way in which the museum as a whole is run. A long series of most eminent men have occupied the full-time paid position of Director of the museum, but the direction of departments is offered as a coveted position to equally eminent men whose livelihood is derived elsewhere. While the coin department has a small permanent staff of learned numismatists, its direction lies in the hands of one of the university dons, at present an eminent historian and numismatist.

One has pleasant recollections of the late Director of the Fitzwilliam walking over from his residence a few yards away in his carpet slippers for a friendly word, and the Director of the coin department pedalling round from his college on a typical university bicycle. But let not this homely atmosphere deceive. Security precautions are of the tightest.

In Glasgow University are housed the great collections of the eighteenth century surgeon, William Hunter and of Thomas Coats, whose family name appears on so many reels of cotton and silk threads in daily household use. Both are of outstanding numismatic importance. Students may view any parts of them in which they may be interested by appointment. The Scottish national collection is housed in Edinburgh where, again, it may be seen by appointment.

A section of the Stockholm Museum's Coin Department

Space will not allow a detailed list of the many other museums in Britain where fine coins may be seen. Important collections exist at Manchester and Leeds, in the Pitt Rivers Museum and at Salisbury. In almost any museum in Britain those interested should not fail to ask what coins the museum holds. In Birmingham, where one would expect a largely 'industrial' interest, the coin collection is a feature, while small museums like the Cuming Museum, Walworth (London), the Prittlewell Museum, Southend-on-Sea and Hartlebury Castle, Worcestershire, can contain numismatic surprises.

The financial power of many of the museums in the United States of America has enabled some of them to build collections of the first importance. Here again many have their foundation in gifts or permanent loan exhibitions. The Cleveland Museum has a fine collection of English gold coins on loan from a local collector. The Boston Museum recently purchased a find of Roman gold coins of such value that its cost lay beyond the finances of museums in Britain. The Seattle Art Museum has a fine collection of Greek coins on loan from a student collector which was featured in a recent catalogue, produced for the museum in London.

The coin collection of the Paris Mint and (*below*) a medal showing an exterior view of the Mint

120

In New York the American Numismatic Society maintains a collection of world importance, probably the only serious rival in depth of coverage to that of the British Museum. The collection is particularly strong in modern coins. It has an unusual feature: it is a 'teaching' collection. Something should be said about the British National Numismatic Congress and the British Association of Numismatic Societies' Study Group. Both these function to teach something of the numismatics within the confines of their financial abilities. The American Society is well enough endowed to be able to invite eminent numismatists to speak and teach at the Society's Summer Seminar each year.

Yet Europe will always be the foundation of numismatic studies. Aside from ancient China, coins were born in Europe and from Europe, unlike ancient China, they spread to the rest of the world. To Europe the student of pure numismatics must ultimately come. In Holland and Belgium, in Italy, Greece and Germany, in Spain and France are the collections which the student must see. In these countries, no less than in Britain, can the genuine 'period' collections of coins be found and studied in depth.

Three Salisbury 17th-century tokens (enlarged). Simon Rolfe (*left*) was a city burgess, and Roger Godfrey (*top, right*) a butcher.

The money of the people

Reference has been made to British copper coinage and its inadequacy before 1797. By the reign of Elizabeth I, a need for a minor coinage was felt and this could not be met with the customary coinage metal, silver. A series of patterns for a copper coinage of halfpence, pennies and, possibly, two-pences appeared, but no such pieces went into circulation.

James I issued licences to certain friends at court to issue minor copper pieces and from this arose a series of small copper farthing tokens. These continued to be struck during the reign of Charles I. The supply was always inadequate and many forgeries appeared.

During the Commonwealth and Protectorate period following the Civil War tradesmen and later some municipalities took matters into their own hands and issued a large number of private farthing, halfpenny and penny tokens during the period 1649-72. These pieces were mainly of copper and brass. Since the exclusive royal prerogative of coining in these metals had ended with the execution of Charles I, a loophole appeared to exist in the coinage law. This, and the fact that the need for such minor coinage was urgent, caused the tokens almost to become a recognized issue. Many collectors include them in their cabinet on this account. They are usually referred to as the Seventeenth Century Tokens.

Their main collecting interest lies in the fact that the issuers put their own names and their places of business on their tokens by way of inscription, while in the centre, part of the arms of their trade or a trade symbol appeared. Thus in Huntingdon there appeared a halfpenny token reading, obverse, WILLIAM LAMBE AT THE with an oak tree in the centre, reverse, IN HVNTINGTON 1668 and HIS HALF PENY in the centre. Lambe probably owned the Royal Oak inn, its name a reference to the Boscobel Oak in which Charles II hid when escaping from England after the Battle of Worcester.

Various cataloguers have classified the thousands of tokens under counties and towns, so that they are easily dealt with by the collector. They provide a great deal of interesting local historical reference and colour. Practically all the important trades –

More 17th-century tokens. The 1st, 2nd and 4th are from the Isle of Wight, the 3rd and 5th from Salisbury.

bakers, tallowchandlers, grocers, mercers, booksellers, weavers, haberdashers and many more – are represented, while the many Royal Oak, King's Head, Crown, Three Crowns and Ship inns may well refer to the royalist cause. So numerous are the series as a whole that some collectors specialize in seventeenth-century tokens alone. With some nine or ten thousand issuers there is obviously plenty of scope for such specialization and the series contains some very rare pieces. London alone had some 3,500 different issues, all of considerable local interest. Usually round, pieces were also struck on square, diamond, octagonal and heart-shaped flans. When a regal copper coinage was finally started in 1672 a Royal Proclamation forbade the further issue and use of such tokens.

Even after 1672 the copper coinage provided by the government was quite inadequate and was extensively forged. Moreover the issue was not continuous but lapsed at intervals. Traders therefore took the matter into their own hands again and began to issue copper tokens, and the series usually now known as the Eighteenth Century Tokens was gradually built up.

Their appearance partly coincided with the work on

A selection of designs on 18th-century tokens. These tokens are from England, Scotland (*bottom, centre*) and Ireland (*bottom, right*).

English tokens of the late 18th century. The illustration of the machinery token (*right*) is enlarged.

improved coining machinery that Boulton was carrying out. In 1787 he issued the first of the series for the Parys Mines Company. Other manufacturers took up what was soon found to be a profitable trade and many hundreds of issues resulted. Forgers also found it profitable to climb on this particular band wagon; it was also somewhat less risky than forging the regal coinage.

The majority of the tokens in this series are halfpennies but there are quite a large number of pennies and even a shilling issued in Basingstoke. The improvements in coining methods resulted in pieces of good shape and reasonably accurate weight. This, and their larger size when compared with the seventeenth-century series, made possible some most interesting local issues. Many of these show buildings of interest, engineering achievements such as canals or the famous 'inclined plane' at Ketley – a primitive form of hauling up an artificial slope. There are many ships, portraits of famous people, town arms and the like. Again a series of considerable size in which some collectors specialize exclusively.

H. A. Seaby's catalogue of the series classifies them into: (1) genuine trade tokens, (2) tokens struck for general circulation and sold by weight, usually with no issuer's name, (3)

Trade tokens illustrated many aspects of local life and social activity.
This 1811 penny (enlarged) shows a Cornish mining scene.

advertising tokens, with usually no mark of value but with a
name, address and trade stated, (4) tokens struck for collectors, (5) private tokens issued by collectors themselves
and (6) forgeries, which fall under a series of sub-divisions.

Though item 4 contains tokens specially provided by manufacturers to stimulate what was a fashionable hobby and not
pieces struck for serious monetary use (as items 1 and 2), the
result is of considerable interest to the collector of the series.
In this section are some very superior pieces, including a
series by Kempson showing famous buildings: rather like a
series of cigarette cards dealing with one particular subject.

Both this series and the previous seventeenth-century issues
offer possibilities for various forms of specialized collecting.
Trades, buildings, portraits, animals and so forth all form
individual series.

Tokens died away once more with the appearance of the
Boulton and Watt regal 'cartwheel' issues and the copper
coinage which followed them in 1799, 1806 and 1807. Then
copper began to rise in price and by 1808 was selling at about

English tokens: among them, a man at a loom (*top, left*), a sailing barge (*top, right*) and a mail coach halfpenny (*bottom, centre*)

£200 a ton. This led to the illegal melting down of copper coinage, to such an extent that a shortage occurred, firstly in the growing industrial areas of the Midlands and the North and later over much of the country. By 1811 the shortage was such that there was again brought into being a series of private tokens, now known as the Nineteenth Century series. Many of these were issued in and around Birmingham and were soon in use over much of the country.

In this series there are more pennies than halfpennies. Once again they have a considerable local interest. Some of the pieces show machinery used in the early days of the industrial revolution while buildings, animals and coats of arms are frequent. As with the previous series they have been catalogued under counties and towns or under the names of firms who used them.

Nothing official was done to prevent their circulation till pieces began to be issued for which the issuers would not pay the equivalent in legal tender, as in theory at any rate token issuers promised to do. The issue was then stopped by an Act of Parliament in 1817 which declared the tokens illegal.

(*Top*) medal commemorating the defeat of the Spanish Armada, 1588.
(*Bottom*) pinchbeck medal marking the Battle of Breslau, 1757.

History in metal

So far we have been looking at coinage, its long history, its metals and its collecting interest. We have seen how it has recorded history and how history has produced coinage.

There is, however, a more direct way in which some parts of history have been recorded in metal: the commemorative medal.

It has been shown by various historians that the Romans issued coins and medallions which commemorated events in their history, and that they used coinage for propaganda purposes. Modern governments have used coinage to commemorate important events in history, giving rise to various commemorative issues, such as the coronation crown of Elizabeth II and the later Churchill crown.

From the general idea of commemorating history on coins there grew up the idea of commemorating important events and people on medals. The artists of the Italian Renaissance produced many fine works of art in medallic form and the idea continued to develop. From such various origins came the commemorative medal as we now know it. Very broadly, coinage gave rise through various divergences both to the commemorative medal and to the medal awarded for services in battle or to the State.

The commemorative medal has a collecting interest that is all its own, one which is quite aside from coin collecting and which is full of interest for the collector who appreciates a direct approach to history through numismatics.

The striking, as opposed to the casting, of commemorative medals presupposes a minting technique that can deal with large flans of metal and strike them successfully with a design. The alternative is to cast such pieces of large size. This was the method employed by the medallists of the Italian Renaissance period. Usually cast pieces have a rough appearance and need some after-treatment when they have left the mould. The Italian artists rubbed off the roughness with sandpaper and used graving tools to bring up the relief of the main portrait or subject.

It is perhaps no coincidence that some of the first commemorative medals struck in Britain appeared in the reign of

Reward given after the defeat of the Spanish Armada

Edward VI. It was in this reign that the first large silver coins produced by the hammer, the crowns of 1551-53, were produced. Mint technicians now had the increased knowledge of how to deal with large and thick flans of metal. Some commemorative medals had appeared during the reign of Edward's father, Henry VIII, as well as during some earlier reigns, but they were not numerous. So far as Britain is concerned the commemorative medal is considered to have come into being in the reign of Henry VIII (1509-46).

Thus the striking of commemorative medals in Britain had become possible in time to record the defeat of the Spanish Armada, 1588, though a number of pieces recording this event were also struck in Holland. For some centuries Britain and Holland both produced commemorative medals of British interest. Striking medals still had its technical difficulties for some time to come, and large pieces were frequently produced by striking two thin silver flans, one for each side of the medal and joining them together with a silver rim. Such medals were being produced at least till the Restoration of Charles II, and some very fine examples give pictorial scenes of contemporary events in high relief. A particularly fine piece of this type, made in Holland, records the embarkation of Charles II in Holland for his voyage to Dover and his restoration to the British throne in 1660.

The general improvement in minting methods, not only in Britain but in Europe as a whole, made it possible at least by the middle of the seventeenth century actually to strike medals of considerable size in gold, silver and bronze. The large silver medal commemorating the 1667 Peace of Breda may perhaps be taken as typical of the size of medal that could now be struck.

It will have been noted that the various medals so far mentioned were issued to record some historic event of importance and thus were a form of political propaganda as well as works of art. The two purposes have frequently run together.

In Britain, Queen Anne's reign (1702-14), with its wars against the French and Spanish, produced one of the really large series of commemorative medals featuring national events. Many of these were the work of the talented medallist

(*Above*) medal commemorating the opening of the Liverpool and Manchester Railway, 1830. (*Below*) one of many medals struck to mark man's first landing on the moon, this one was produced in two sizes in gold, silver and platinum.

John Croker. He had been preceded by the brothers Abraham and Thomas Simon and the Roettiers, who produced many fine medals of artistic and historic importance. Croker recorded in medallic form not only such peaceful events as accessions and coronations but provided a record of the wars of his period. Such actions as the Battle of Blenheim, 1704, the Capture of Gibraltar in the same year, the Battle of Ramillies and that of Almenara, the attempted invasion of Scotland and the cities and islands which fell to the allies are all faithfully recorded, mostly as reverse designs for medals the obverse of which usually carried the portrait of the simple, homely, buxom Queen Anne.

With so skilful an artist as Croker available the government of the day pushed his powers to the limit in recording as a form of propaganda which the public could understand the great military and civil events of the reign.

Croker lived on into the next two reigns and was thus able to record the arrival of George I in Britain, his entry into London, his coronation and some of the events of his reign. He produced a portrait

(*Above*) medal struck after the English victories over the Dutch, 1653. (*Opposite page, from the top*) capture of Gibraltar, 1783; military badge of the Earl of Manchester, 1643; reverse, George V Coronation medal, 1911; obverse, Battle of Oudenoude medal, 1708.

medal of Sir Isaac Newton, sometime Master of the Royal Mint, as well as the coronation medal of George II. The Simon, Roettier, Croker period was a high-spot in the art of the medallist in Britain.

By the latter part of the reign of George III, the industrial revolution was gaining momentum. The power of steam applied, as we have seen, to minting, gave rise to a profusion of commemorative medals. As well as political events, medals now began to record something of the mechanical and industrial achievements of the age. We have medallic record of the opening of the Liverpool and Manchester Railway in 1830, with views of contemporary trains passing over the great viaducts, which in themselves were outstanding engineering achievements. Medals show us the portraits of the two Stephensons, father and son, of Mark and Isambard Kingdom Brunel, and of the building of the Thames Tunnel, the world's first underwater public road, completed in 1843. They show us the early steamships, such as the *Great Eastern* and many more such events.

A record exists of the Napoleonic Wars and the achieve-

ments of Wellington in a series of medals issued as a set.
Wellington himself was portrayed on an immense variety of
medals. Coronations were recorded in medallic form as far
back as the reign of Edward VI and James I, from which reign
coronation medals were issued by the Royal Mint till the reign
of George VI. The Jubilees of Queen Victoria and George V
were medallically recorded, as was the Great Exhibition of
1851. During this, the world's first great industrial and cultural
exhibition, exhibitors, judges and jurors were awarded finely
struck medals, usually in bronze.

During the short reign of William IV (1830-37), and the
long reign of Victoria (1837-1901), the commemorative medal
reached its zenith of mass production. Apart from the Royal
Mint, whose production was always carefully restrained,
private medallists, many in the Birmingham area, poured forth
medals to commemorate anything and everything. As is not
unusual, artistic standards suffered with mass production.

With the invention of the camera and the picture postcard,
followed by the cinema and television, the spate of commem-

(*Opposite*) Charles II's head on a medal struck to commemorate the Peace of Breda, 1677 (enlarged). (*Above, left*) the death of Nelson at Trafalgar in 1805 was marked by this copper medal. (*Right*) a medal of Anne of Denmark, consort of James I of England, probably struck for their coronation in 1603.

orative medals died. Events were now being recorded or seen as they happened. The propaganda purpose of the medal had now been partly lost. Though far less were struck those which appeared were returning to a higher artistic standard. By the reign of George V, the commemorative medal had reverted to its rightful place as an object of artistic merit and historic importance. Those now being struck are usually produced in small numbers and record such important events as the 900th year of Westminster Abbey (1966), the centenary of the London and Birmingham Railway, the world's first trunk line (1938), the Jubilee of George V (1935), the commissioning of the greatest liner of them all, the Queen Mary (1936) and portraits of contemporary persons of importance.

The selection of medals so far given has been taken quite at random from among the thousands available to collectors and has no important significance as a record. But enough has been said to show that the commemorative medal is a collecting theme of great interest. It is one in which many collectors have specialized in past time. It suffered a decline in collecting interest in the twentieth century but is now rapidly gaining ground as the price of coins continues to rise. A word might therefore be said on some aspects of medal collecting.

The commemorative medal is struck in a variety of metals. Gold, silver and bronze are the most usual. With the latter metal a really pleasing piece can be produced. The bronze medals in the Queen Anne series already referred to as well as those struck at the French mint at the present day are fine examples of what can be done with this particular metal. As medals proliferated, pewter or 'white metal' was extensively used. This wears badly, soon tarnishes and, unless well cared for, becomes rough and unpleasant both in appearance and to the touch. In its finest state, however, it can be really sparkling and attractive. Medals are also struck in platinum, nickel, aluminium and almost any of the coinage metals which we discussed in a previous chapter.

The housing of medals needs special consideration. They tend to be larger than coins, 1–4 inches diameter being fairly common. A special cabinet is therefore required in which to keep them as they will not fit into coin-size piercings. The custom-built cabinets now available in the coinage field can also be supplied with open trays in which medals can be kept. Since the sizes of medals are so varied such trays are the obvious solution for the collector. Even so, medals placed in an open tray tend to slip about, knock together and become disarranged. A horizontal strip of thin wood placed at intervals across the tray will at least keep the medals in a straight line. Unless considerable expense can be accepted not much more can be offered by a medal cabinet.

As items of artistic merit a small collection of medals can be displayed in a glass-topped showcase. One sees examples in some of the great houses in Britain of this method of display. Though attractive, such methods of display can only contain a small collection – few collectors live in large 'stately homes' in this day and age.

Apart from the problems of how best to keep or display a collection of commemorative medals these pieces do not pose many problems. Unlike coins, which pass from hand to hand and thus become worn, the medal is an exhibition piece, and is thus usually in extremely fine, or better condition.

Save in certain exceptions which prove the rule the collector should not accept anything below extremely fine condition when he adds to his collection.

One of the exceptions is a series known as the Vernon medals. These were struck in large numbers by Christopher Pinchbeck, a clock and toy maker of Fleet Street who had invented the gilt-covered base metal – brass alloyed with zinc – which still retains his name. Pinchbeck struck many medals in his metal to record Admiral Vernon's boast that he could take Porto-Bello with only six ships. According to the Dictionary of English History Vernon failed to take Porto-Bello 'from an insufficiency of force'. According to Pinchbeck 'he took Porto-Bello with six ships only'. Be that as it may, medals in Pinchbeck metal recording Vernon's achievements exist in large numbers. The gilt soon wore off the gingerbread, so that a Pinchbeck medal in really first class state, glittering in all its gilt covering, is hard to find. Collectors of this particular series mainly accept specimens in poor condition, with the gilt rubbed off. The exception that proves the rule: as a series commemorative medals should not be accepted below EF condition.

Medal ribands

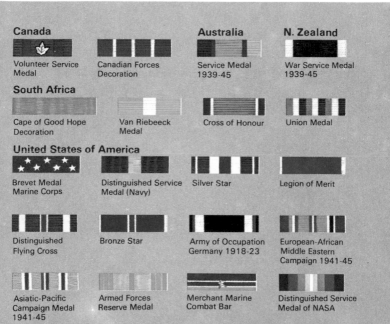

Canada

Volunteer Service Medal

Canadian Forces Decoration

Australia

Service Medal 1939-45

N. Zealand

War Service Medal 1939-45

South Africa

Cape of Good Hope Decoration

Van Riebeeck Medal

Cross of Honour

Union Medal

United States of America

Brevet Medal Marine Corps

Distinguished Service Medal (Navy)

Silver Star

Legion of Merit

Distinguished Flying Cross

Bronze Star

Army of Occupation Germany 1918-23

European-African Middle Eastern Campaign 1941-45

Asiatic-Pacific Campaign Medal 1941-45

Armed Forces Reserve Medal

Merchant Marine Combat Bar

Distinguished Service Medal of NASA

For bravery and service

The custom of awarding medals for bravery in war or for service to the monarch or the state may be said to have had its origins, so far as Britain is concerned, in about the reign of Henry VIII. It could almost be said that the idea grew out of that of wearing dress ornaments, since medals were on occasion given by the king as a mark of friendship or esteem and worn by the recipients on a gold chain as an addition to dress. Many of these pieces were as large as commemorative medals. The Armada Medal, mentioned in the previous chapter, is considered by Mayo as being intended for wear as an ornament. Thus a slight origin-connection exists between the two types of medal.

By the time we reach the Civil Wars of Charles I, oval silver and silver-gilt badges were being struck, usually with the king's portrait on the obverse. These, it is said, were in some instances given by the king to his supporters. The loyalists of high rank no doubt wore them in the field of battle. It is possible that the king may have given some of these badges for particularly brilliant or brave actions. After the defeat of the Royalists no doubt many of them wore these badges beneath their clothing as a mark of their continued loyalty to the throne and to the exiled king, Charles II.

The awarding of medals as we now know them, consisting of a metal disc, star, cross or other suitable shape to be worn by the recipient suspended from a riband – medallists frequently use the old spelling of ribbon – is not of great antiquity. Such pieces are frequently called decorations and one hears such phrases as 'he was decorated by the Queen' for some particular act.

The Hon. East India Company decorated some of its servants with medals suspended from ribands, to be worn on suitable occasions. This rich and powerful company had at one time its own armed ships and military force with which to back its trading ventures and to maintain discipline in the territories which it gradually acquired or in the territorial concessions which it was granted. Ultimately the activities of the company, which also had its own coinage for a considerable period, resulted in the Empire of India. That is another story, typical of the many encountered in coin and medal collecting.

The Victoria Cross, instituted in 1856 at the end of the Crimean War, is awarded to members of the armed forces for conspicuous bravery. Britain's highest and most venerated military award for bravery, it has been won by servicemen throughout the Commonwealth, most recently by an Australian in Vietnam.

British orders and decorations. (*Opposite page, top left*): military badge of the Order of Merit, founded by Edward VII in 1902. (*Top right*) military, Knight Commander and Companion Badge of the Most Honourable Order of the Bath. (*Centre*) collar of the Most Distinguished Order of St Michael and St George. (*This page, top*) Crimean War Medal, Queen's South Africa Medal. (*Bottom*) Waterloo Medal, Naval General Service Medal, 1793-1840.

Distinguished Flying
Cross (Britain)

Belgian War
Cross 1940

Atlantic Star
(Britain)

The naval battle of the Glorious First of June, 1794, in which
Lord Howe and the British defeated a French fleet 400 miles
out in the Atlantic, was the first occasion on which awards
were made on a regular system. A gold medal, design by an
Italian, Thomas Pingo, was given to admirals and captains who
had particularly distinguished themselves.

Unfortunately, not everyone who should perhaps have
received a medal was given one, and some ill-feeling was
caused. However, the first step had been taken towards the
now almost universal system in the world's armed services
of giving awards for service in battle.

USA Meritorious
Service Medal,
Merchant Marine

German Iron
Cross 1939,
second class

USA Navy
Cross

It is not certain if the action of 'John Company' in awarding medals inspired the British government to follow up the idea, but sometime after the Battle of Waterloo in 1815, the Waterloo medal was instituted and awarded. It consisted of a circular silver disc suspended from a riband, was awarded to participants and was intended for wear by them on suitable occasions. The medal bore the effigy of the Prince Regent, not that of the king, George III. The riband was red with blue edges.

In 1848 the Naval General Service Medal was instituted, and took a similar form. Another feature of Victoria's reign was the granting of medals to the survivors of actions on sea or land to as far back as 1793. Thus the system of decorations as we know it may be said to have come into being.

The various wars which followed, the Crimean, South African, the First and Second World Wars, the fighting on the North West Frontier of India, in Aden, the Far East and many similar conflicts brought into being medallic awards. Broadly, the Navy, Army and the Royal Air Force have particular awards of their own, such as the Naval General Service Medal, the Military General Service Medal and the Distinguished Flying Cross, to name but three of the many.

There are medals for certain special campaigns, for polar exploration, for service with the police force, for life-saving and great bravery in

(*Top*) civil badge of the British Empire Medal.
(*Bottom*) the George Cross, instituted in 1940 mainly as an award for civilians, for acts of the greatest heroism.

some civil field of action. Such medals and many more are awarded for services rendered in many ways.

It was not very long after decorations in their present form were instituted that bars or clasps were added to the riband of certain basic awards for service in some particular action. The Queen's South Africa Medal, for example, awarded for service in the South African War, can have bars for Cape Colony, Tugela Heights, Orange Free State, the Relief of Ladysmith, the Transvaal, and Laing's Nek. A soldier wearing a medal with these bars saw service in all these places in South Africa and his service was thus recorded.

It will be seen, therefore, that the collector of campaign medals, as such decorations are frequently called, is soon in very close touch with the men to whom the medals in his collection were awarded. There is thus a personal feeling in medal collecting that does not exist for the collector of coins. A feeling of respect is felt by the medal collector for the brave soldiers, often long dead, whose medals come into his cabinet. The medal collector is not a type of vulture, acquiring the medals of

some hero of the past simply for profit. He respects and honours the men whose deeds of bravery and service earned the medals in his collection, thus keeping alive the gallantry of the soldiers of the past.

The services rendered by many who were awarded medals are recorded in the rolls of the regiment and in certain cases in the London Gazette. Here is an entry in that important publication recording the service of a certain Acting Corporal Hart which gained him the Military Medal.

'London Gazette, 17th June, 1943. In the attack on the Mareth Line (North Africa) on March 20th 1943, Corporal Hart was a stretcher bearer Corporal with "A" Company advancing through a Wadi to attack an enemy position. Extremely heavy enemy artillery mortar and machine-gun fire, amongst which the reverse platoon of the company was almost entirely disabled. Corporal Hart organized and led the work of his stretcher bearers with such efficiency that although several of his men had been put out of action, he was mainly responsible for maintaining clearance for the casualties for the company, and also for two other companies who were simultaneously passing through the Wadi and whose stretcher bearers had become casualties. His conduct throughout was directly responsible for saving a very large number of our troops, who, having become casualties, were in great danger of being killed by artillery fire.'

Accounts such as this give some idea of how much the 'man behind the medal' becomes a personality to the medal collector. One of the casualties saved by Hart might have been your father, your husband or your son.

Medals also occur in groups, telling the story of many years service in different parts of the world. Often there are foreign decorations, in their appropriate place in the group, adding further to the interest.

On the rare occasions where a man wins the same decoration twice, such as the DFC, some form of addition is made to his

The Most Noble Order of the Garter: the star of the Order (*top*), the collar and badge (the 'George') and the Garter. This is the world's oldest historically documented order of chivalry.

first award. For being 'mentioned in dispatches', itself an honour, an additional symbol is added to the riband. The colours of the riband signify something of the purpose and origin of the medal. The riband of the Africa Star is basically of sand colour, for the desert. A broad stripe of red stands for the army. Another of dark blue for the navy. A third of light blue indicates the air force. All of these forces took part in the African campaigns of World War II for which the medal was instituted.

Among all the gay colours of British medal ribands that of the supreme award for gallantry, the rare Victoria Cross, is the simplest of them all. The medal itself is made from bronze cannon and is as simple as its award is great. Still rarer as yet is the George Cross, instituted by George VI in World War II. Only a few have so far been awarded.

Contact with the person to whom a medal was awarded

(*Above*) Czechoslovak Order of the White Lion: military 2nd and 3rd class badge of the Order. (*Below*) British Distinguished Service Order, awarded to commissioned officers for especial service in action.

is established through his name being engraved on his medal, usually on the rim. There are various snags in metal collecting. One of them is the unofficial renaming of a medal – a medal named to a person who never received it; another is bars added for actions in which the recipient never took part. These are typical. Many other such points must be considered by the medal collector. There are several standard reference works dealing with the whole subject of medal collecting, together with a profusion of books on medals as a whole.

The collecting of medals brings up once more the question of how they should be kept. Custom-built cabinets are available, with open trays in which the medals with their ribands can be set out to advantage. Some collectors have medals mounted and framed, to hang like pictures. Usually each frame contains the medals of one particular war or series of actions. Some collectors even go further and add a map, or a picture of soldiers typical of the period, or of the man who was awarded

The Swedish military Order of the Sword, the star of the Grand Cross of which is illustrated below, has its origins in an organization founded by King Gustavus Vasa I in 1522

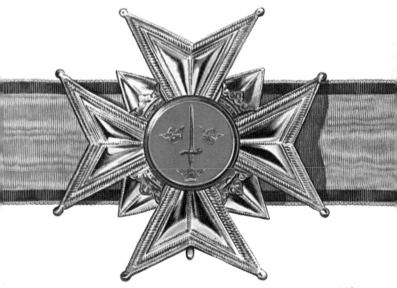

Malta, Knights Order
of Honour and Devotion

some special group of medals.

The cleaning of medals and the question of replacing the riband by a nice new colourful piece is one of personal choice. Many collectors prefer to keep the 'original' riband though, if the recipient wore the medal very often, it is doubtful if the riband is the original piece. If the medal has seen much wear it will certainly have been cleaned many times. Once or twice more will do little harm. Save in special cases, there is no reason why a collection of medals should not present a clean and bright appearance. No warrior appears on parade with dirty medals.

Orders of Chivalry and Civil Decorations are a series in themselves, one in which collectors also take an active interest. Usually the Orders of Chivalry are not available to the collector. The insignia generally has to be returned to the Central Chancery of the Orders of Knighthood on the death of the recipient or, if retained by the family, may not be sold.

The insignia of such orders is often elaborate and costly. It frequently consists of a highly decorated chain of gold or silver-gilt and an enamelled breast star. In some

Grand cross of the French Legion of Honour (Republican period).
The Legion of Honour, instituted by Napoleon in 1804, has become
the most honoured decoration of France and its five grades can
be gained by servicemen and civilians.

instances, such as that of the famous Duke of Wellington, the
insignia is further enriched by the addition of diamonds or
other precious stones as a mark of additional respect. Decorations and orders are frequently showered on such famous
people by grateful governments. The many given to the Duke
can be seen in the Wellington Museum at Apsley House, a
calm oasis in the middle of the roar of traffic at Hyde Park
Corner in London. Others find their way into the regimental
museums or specialized museums, such as the National Maritime at Greenwich, where many of Lord Nelson's awards and
decorations may be seen.

In some cases the number of people who may be admitted
to an Order at any one time is limited. Often there is an elaborate, ancient and colourful ceremony when a new member is
admitted. Such a ceremony surrounds the admissions to the
Most Noble Order of the Garter whose annual procession to

The third highest state order of Imperial Russia, the Order of the White Eagle, with swords. Originally a Polish order, it was taken over by the czars after the partition of Poland.

St George's Chapel, Windsor Castle, is a splendid occasion.

This order, of the greatest antiquity, held by many to be the world's highest honour, was instituted by Edward III in about 1348. Originally it was the highest reward for military merit.

Other orders of the highest importance are the Most Ancient and Most Noble Order of the Thistle, probably founded about 809 and revived on a regular foundation in 1687. The Most Honourable Order of the Bath grew out of the custom that those about to be knighted purified their souls by fasting and prayer and their bodies by bathing. The Order of the Bath was created by George I in 1725, but the custom from which it obtains its title dates back to at least William I. The Most

Distinguished Order of St Michael and St George was founded on 27 April 1818, by the Prince Regent on behalf of George III. The previous year Malta had come under the British Sovereign and seven Ionian islands were placed under British protection. The new order was intended as a reward for Ionians and Maltese who by most meritorious service had shown outstanding loyalty to the Crown. It was to become one of Britain's highest awards for merit, however, being awarded to successful diplomatists and heads of state.

The Royal Victorian Order was founded by Queen Victoria in 1896, as a personal award for which she herself paid. It is awarded for important personal service to the monarch. The Most Excellent Order of the British Empire was instituted by George V during World War I, with awards suitable for all ranks of the community, five classes of award being provided. This was an indication of awards becoming more democratic;

Breast star of the Siamese Order of the White Elephant, best-known Siamese order. It was founded in 1861.

as was the institution in 1902 of the Order of Merit and the Order of the Companions of Honour.

Treated as a personal award of the Sovereign, the Order of Merit is often considered to be the most coveted distinction among British orders. It is awarded to those who have given particularly outstanding service in the armed forces or exceptionally meritorious service towards the advancement of art, literature and science. Thus there are Prime Ministers, poets, authors, historians, scientists, an aeroplane designer, an architect and a sculptor among those on whom the Order has been conferred. It carries no title but simply the letters OM after the recipient's name. The Order has one grade and is limited to twenty-four members.

The wearing of insignia for various civil purposes is also of considerable antiquity. It probably has its foundation in the general idea of decoration as an indication of authority

Collar and badge of the Scottish Most Ancient Order of the Thistle. The figure on the medallion is St Andrew, holding his saltire cross. Thistles and branches of rue form the collar

Egypt Medal
1882-9

British Korea
Medal, 1950-53

together with the idea of public esteem for the wearer. Lord Mayors and mayors of cities and towns have a chain and badge of office during their mayoralty. This they wear on all official occasions, be it at council meetings or at the opening of a church bazaar. The Freemasons have a whole hierarchy of Orders of their own, with many grades and classes. Many other societies have insignia in various forms. Broadly the purpose of the whole idea is to mark appreciation of some service given by them for the public good.

Military and civil decorations, medals and awards are a rich collecting theme, with many facets and many avenues of specialized collecting. As with coins, there are both common and very rare pieces. An immense amount of background history lies behind any part of the subject. As with any serious form of collecting be it coins, medals, pictures or any subject of equal significance, the collector will be greatly enriched as the years pass and the collection grows. Herein lies a richness far greater than just that of the increase in the value of the collection.

BOOKS TO READ

Among the many books written about coins and medals, the following will give readers a wide coverage of the subject. They are generally available from libraries, booksellers and publishers.

American War Medals and Decorations by E. E. Kerrigan. Viking Press, New York.

British Copper Coins and their Values by P. J. Seaby and M. Bussell. Seaby, London, 5th edition 1967.

Catalog of Modern World Coins by R. S. Yeoman. Whitman, Wisconsin.

The Coinage of Ancient Britain by R. P. Mack. Spink and Seaby, London, 2nd edition 1964.

Collecting Medals and Decorations by Alec A. Purves. Seaby, London, 1968.

The Crown Pieces of Great Britain and the British Commonwealth by H. W. A. Linecar. Spink, London.

English Hammered Coinage by J. J. North. Spink, London, 2 vols. 1960-63.

English Trade Tokens by P. Mathias. Abelard, London, 1962.

Greek Coins by Charles Seltman. Methuen, London, 2nd edition 1955.

Greek Coins and Cities by Norman Davis. Spink, London, 1967.

A Guide Book of English Coins by K. E. Bresset. Whitman, Wisconsin.

A Guide Book of United States Coins by R. S. Yeoman. Whitman, Wisconsin.

The Handbook of the Coinage of Great Britain and Ireland in the British Museum by H. A. Grueber, revised by Dr. J. P. C. Kent, Ian Stewart, Patrick Finn and H. W. A. Linecar. Spink, London, 1970.

Medals and Decorations of the British Army and Navy by J. H. Mayo. London, 1897.

The Milled Coinage of England, 1662-1946 by H. W. A. Linecar. Spink, London, 1950.

The Mint by Sir John Craig. Cambridge University Press, 1953.

Orders and Decorations by Václav Mérićka. Hamlyn, London, 1967.

Orders, Medals and Decorations by Paul Hieronymussen. Blandford Press, London, 1967.

The Provincial Token Coinage of the 18th Century by R. Dalton and S. H. Hamer. Seaby, London, 1967.

Ribbons and Medals by H. Taprell Dorling. George Philip, London.

Roman Coins by Harold Mattingly. Methuen, London, 1955.

The Standard Catalogue of British Orders, Decorations and Medals, with valuations, by E. C. Joslin. Spink, London, 1969.

The Story of Money by A. H. Quiggin. Methuen, London, 1956.

INDEX

SOME OTHER TITLES IN THIS SERIES